Native American Myths and Legends

Native American Myths and Legends

ARCTURUS

ARCTURUS

© 2018 Arcturus Holdings Limited

ISBN: 978-1-78828-834-7
AD005601US

Printed in China

2 4 6 8 10 9 7 5 3 1

Contents

Creation Myths

10 ◆ **Kuterasan and Creation (Apache)**

16 ◆ **The Discovery of the Upper World (Jicarillas)**

20 ◆ **Creation Myth (Navajo)**

35 ◆ **The Bird of Ages (Cree)**

42 ◆ **Alaskan Creation Myths (Inuit)**

46 ◆ **The Bringing of the Light by Raven (Inuit)**

49 ◆ **The First Totem Pole (Kwakiutl)**

52 ◆ **How the Old Man Above Created the World (Shastika)**

53 ◆ **Old Mole's Creation (Shastika)**

54 ◆ **How Qawaneca Created the World (Chemetunne)**

56 ◆ **Blackfoot Genesis (Blackfoot)**

64 ◆ **The Creation of the World (Pima)**

66 ◆ **Beginning of Newness (Zuni)**

71 ◆ **The Men of Early Times (Zuni)**

72 ◆ **Spider's Creation (Sia)**

74 ◆ **How Silverfox Created the World (Atsugewi)**

77 ◆ **Creation of the World (Wyandot)**

80 ◆ **How the People got Five Fingers and Other Stories (Miwok)**

83 ◆ **The Evil Maker (Ojibwa)**

84 ◆ **Legend of the Corn (Arikara)**

88 ◆ **Yo-Sem-i-Te, Large Grizzly Bear (Yosemite)**

Heroes and Tricksters

94 ◆ **The Raven Myth (Inuit)**

104 ◆ **The Flood (Tlingit)**

107 ◆ **How Raven Stole the Lake (Haida)**

109 ◆ **Origin of Light and Fire (Lillooet)**

112 ◆ **Raven's Canoe Men (Haida)**

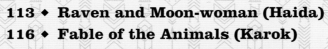

113 ◆ **Raven and Moon-woman (Haida)**

116 ◆ **Fable of the Animals (Karok)**

119 ◆ **How Coyote Stole Fire (Klamath)**

121 ◆ **Origin of the Tribes (Chinook)**

124 ◆ **How Ah-ha'-le Stole the Sun (Miwok)**

128 ◆ **Coyote and Grizzly (Nez Perce)**

130 ◆ **Coyote in the Buffalo Country (Flathead)**

132 ◆ **Coyote and the Salmon (Klamath)**

134 ◆ **How Coyote was Killed (Clatsop)**

135 ◆ **Wiske-djak and the Geese (Algonquin)**

140 ◆ **Wiske-djak and the Partridges (Algonquin)**

142 ◆ **Wiske-djak and Great Beaver (Algonquin)**

144 ◆ **Wek'-wek's search for his father (Miwok)**

152 ◆ **Wek'-wek's search for his sister (Miwok)**

154 ◆ **Wek'-wek's visit to the Underworld People (Miwok)**

156 ◆ **A Legend of Manabozho (Ojibwa)**

159 ◆ **Manabozho in the Fish's Stomach (Ojibwa)**

161 ◆ **The Sun and the Moon (Ojibwa)**

163 ◆ **Manabozho the Wolf (Ojibwa)**

168 ◆ **How Glooscap Found the Summer (Mi'kmaq)**

169 ◆ **How Glooscap Conquered his Enemies (Mi'kmaq)**

176 ◆ **How Glooscap Defeated the Sorcerers (Mi'kmaq)**

179 ◆ **How Glooscap was Conquered by Wasis (Mi'kmaq)**

180 ◆ **Origin of the Thunder Bird (Klamath)**

181 ◆ **Turtle and the Thunder Bird (Ojibwa)**

183 ◆ **Why Lightning Strikes the Trees (Thompson River)**

184 ◆ **The Last of the Thunderbirds (Inuit)**

185 ◆ **The Magic Birth of Nenebuc and His Four Brothers (Ojibwa)**

187 ◆ **Nenebuc Tempers the Wind (Ojibwa)**

189 ◆ **Nenebuc Prepares a Great Feast (Ojibwa)**

190 ◆ **Nenebuc Gets Caught in the Bear's Skull (Ojibwa)**

191 ◆ **Picture Credits**

Introduction

Throughout the world myths and legends have developed to help explain our role in the universe. They tell us about our origins and the origins of the world we live in, explain why events happen as they do, often through supernatural beings or the machinations of fate, and provide us with lessons on how to live our lives. The mythology of the indigenous peoples of North America was no different, and yet, in its many iterations, it is still unique.

Many of these legends relate to momentous events—to the creation of the world, to the first man and woman, to the birth of fire and the origins of the wind, lightning, and the rain. According to the Navajo, the first humans emerged from an underworld to discover a bountiful habitat illuminated by the sun during daytime and the moon at nighttime. Among the various tribes of Alaska, the world begins as an immense expanse of water that is transformed by the actions of intrepid men and women. For the Blackfoot, a deity known as the "Old Man" travels across the prairies creating life as he goes. Unlike many other cultures, most of these creation myths assume the permanence of the world—the world we live in now has evolved or changed from what existed before, but it was rarely created specifically for the benefit of humanity.

Prominent in Native American mythology is the trickster or transformer. At once god, hero, and villain, the trickster is responsible for both providing the necessities that make the life of men possible and the hardships that make life a constant struggle. In the Southwest, the trickster was called Coyote; in the Pacific Northwest, he was called Raven; among the Algonquin peoples of the Great Lakes region, he was called Wiske-djak, and along the Atlantic coast of New England and Canada, he was called Glooscap. Though represented by a variety of different creatures and imbued by their storytellers with a wide range of powers, these characters had much in common with each other. The stories of the sedentary, agricultural peoples of the Eastern seaboard shared more than one would expect with the nomadic tribes of the Great Plains. The stealing of fire, the bringing of light to mankind, and the mischievous competition between the trickster and his enemies are common motifs in all these legends. In a story of the Miwok peoples, Wek'wek the falcon found a wife in the underworld, while in a tale of the Algonquin, Nenebuc, the child of the sun, threatens the West Wind so the people can live in peace.

The tales collected in this volume come from a range of sources, most collected during the 19th century as Victorian travelers feared the disappearance of native cultures with the onset of industrialization. Some chose to write down the tales they heard when visiting native camps and

villages. Others, especially academics in the newly emerging discipline of ethnology, sought out these legends in much the same way the Brothers Grimm had done for German folk tales a century before.

The most famous of these documenters of the so-called "dying race" was Edward Curtis. Curtis was a renowned photographer and ethnologist who spent his life recording the lives of the Native Americans through the lens of his camera. His stunning portraits included in this volume indicate the sheer diversity of cultures present among the first peoples of the continent. In 1906, with the support of J. P. Morgan, Curtis began work on what would become his magnum opus, *The North American Indian*. Over the course of 20 years, he took more than 40,000 photographs of individuals from more than 80 different tribes. Accompanying these images were notes detailing their traditions, ceremonies, foods, housing, clothing, and recreation activities, and in some instances, he even provided biographical sketches of tribal leaders.

These myths and legends represent only a small sample of the countless fables of the Native American peoples. The following tales will inspire and fascinate, and provide unique insight into an enduring culture.

Creation Myths

Kuterasan and Creation (Apache)

There was a time when nothing existed to form the universe—no earth, no sky, and no sun or moon to break the monotony of the illimitable darkness. But as time rolled on, a spot, a thin circular disc no larger than the hand, yellow on one side and white on the other, appeared in midair. Inside the disc sat a bearded man but little larger than a frog, upon whom was to fall the task of creating all things. Kuterastan, The One Who Lives Above, is the name by which he is now known, though some call him Yuadistan, Sky Man.

Kuterastan, as if waking from a long sleep, sat up and rubbed his face and eyes with both hands. Then bending forward, he looked up into the endless darkness, and—lo!—light appeared everywhere above him. He then looked down, and all below became a sea of light. A glance to the east created yellow streaks of dawn, another to the west the saffron tints of the dying day, both soon becoming obscured by numerous clouds of many hues, formed by his looking around and about in all directions.

Again with both hands Kuterastan wiped his eyes and sweating face and, rubbing his hands together as if he were rolling a small pebble between the palms, suddenly parted them with a quick downward fling, and there before him on a shining, vaporless mirage-like cloud sat a little girl no larger than a doll. Kuterastan directed her to stand up, asking where she intended to go, but she replied not. He cleared his vision once more with his hands, then proffered his right hand to the girl, Stenatliha, Woman Without Parents, who grasped it, with the greeting "Whence came you?"

For reply Kuterastan merely repeated her question, adding, "Look to the east, it is light! There will be light in the south, in the west, and in the north." And as she looked she saw light. He then came out upon the cloud.

"Where is the earth?" asked Stenatliha, to which Kuterastan replied by asking:

"Where is the sky?" Then requesting that he be not disturbed, he began to sing: "I am thinking, thinking, thinking, thinking what shall I do next." Four times he thus sang, at the end of the fourth time brushing his face with his hands, which he rubbed briskly together and parted quickly;

CHIEF GERONIMO
APACHE

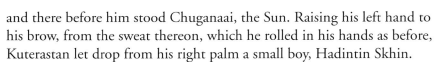

and there before him stood Chuganaai, the Sun. Raising his left hand to his brow, from the sweat thereon, which he rolled in his hands as before, Kuterastan let drop from his right palm a small boy, Hadintin Skhin.

The four sat upon that still cloud for a time as if in reverie, the first to break the silence being he who commenced the creation: "What shall we do next? I do not like this cloud to live upon, but we are to rule and must stay together. How dreary it is here! I wish we had some place to go." And then he set to work again, creating Nacholecho, the Tarantula, who was later to help in completing the earth, and Nokuse, the Big Dipper, whose duty it would be to befriend and to guide. The creation of Nnchidilhkizn, the Wind, Ndidilhkizn, the Lightning Maker, and the clouds in the west to house Ndisagocha, Lightning Rumbler, whom he placed in them at the same time, next occupied his attention. Then turning to Stenatliha, Kuterastan said, "Truly this is not a fit place in which to live; let us make the earth." And so saying he at once began to sing, "I am thinking of the earth, the earth, the earth; I am thinking of the earth," which he repeated four times. As he ceased, Stenatliha, Chuganaai, and Hadintin Skhin each shook hands with him. Sweat from their hands adhered to his. He at once began rubbing his palms, when suddenly there slipped from between them a small brown body, no larger than a bean. Kuterastan kicked it and it expanded; Stenatliha then kicked it and its size further increased; Chuganaai next gave it a severe blow with his foot and it became larger still; a kick from Hadintin Skhin made it greater yet. Nilchidilbkizn, the Wind, was told to go inside and blow outward in all directions. This he did, greatly expanding the dimensions of that body, now so wide that they could hardly see its edge. The Lightning was next directed to exert his strength, so with a terrific flash and roar he penetrated the body to its centre, spreading it still wider. Then Tarantula was called on to assist, and accordingly he started off to the east, spinning a strong black cord, on which he pulled with all his might; another cord of blue was spun out to the south, a third of yellow to the west, and a fourth of glistening white to the north. A mighty pull on each of these stretched the surface of that dark brown body to almost immeasurable size. Finally Kuterastan directed all to cover their eyes with their hands, and when they opened them a moment later they beheld Nigostiin, the Earth, complete in extent. No hills or mountains were there in sight, nothing but a smooth, treeless, reddish-brown plain.

Nilchidribkizn, the Wind, scratched his chest and rubbed his fingers together, when out from between them flew Datilye, the Humming-bird. Datilye was told to make a circuit of the earth and report what he saw. He started off toward the east, circled south, west, north, and back from the east. All was well; the earth was most beautiful, very smooth, and covered with water on the western side.

But the Earth was not still; it kept shifting and rolling and dancing up and down, so Kuterastan made four great posts—colored black, blue, yellow, and white—to support it. Then he directed Stenatliha to sing a song. She sang, "The world is made and will soon sit still." These two then stood and faced Chuganaai and Hadintin Skhin, when into their midst came Ntlchidilbkizn, who dashed away to the cardinal points with the four posts, which he placed under the sides of the earth; and upon them it sat and was still. This pleased Kuterastan, so he sang a song, repeating,

"The world is now made and sits still."

Then Kuterastan began another song, referring to the sky. None existed as yet, and he felt there ought to be one. Four times he chanted the song, at the end of the fourth time spreading his hands wide before him, when lo! there stood twenty-eight men and women ready to help make a sky to cover the earth. He next chanted a song for the purpose of making chiefs for the sky and the earth, and at its close sent Ndidilbkizn, the Lightning Maker, to encircle the world. Ndidilbkizn departed at once, but returned in a short time with three very uncouth persons, two girls and a boy, whom he had found in the sky in a large turquoise bowl. Not one of them had eyes, ears, hair, mouth, nose, or teeth, and though they had arms and legs, they had neither fingers nor toes.

Chuganaai at once sent for Doh, the Fly, to come and erect a kache, or sweat-house. It took but a short time to put up the framework, which Stenatliha covered closely with four heavy clouds: a black cloud on the east, a blue one on the south, a yellow one on the west, and a white one on the north. Out in front of the doorway, at the east, she spread a soft red cloud for a foot-blanket after the sweat. Twelve stones were heated in a fire, and four of them placed in the kache. Kuterastan, Stenatliha, Chuganaai, and Hadintin Skhin each inspected the sweat-house and pronounced it well made. The three newcomers were bidden to enter and were followed by Chuganaai, Nilchidilhkizn, Ndidilbkizn, Nokuse, and Doh. The eight sang songs as their sweat began. Chuganaai led, singing four songs, and each of the others followed in turn with the same number. They had had a good sweat by the time the songs were finished, so Stenatliha removed the black cloud and all came out. She then placed the three strangers on the red-cloud blanket, and under the direction of Kuterastan made for them fingers, toes, mouth, eyes, ears, hair, and nose. Then Kuterastan bade them welcome, making the boy, whom he called Yadilhkih Skhin, Sky Boy, chief of the sky and its people. The second he named Nigostiin Nalin, Earth Daughter, and placed her in charge of the earth and its crops; while to the third, Hadintin Nalin, Pollen Girl, was assigned the care of the health of the earth's people. This duty also devolved upon Hadintin Skhin, but each looks more to the welfare of his own sex than to that of the other.

The earth was smooth, flat, and barren, so Kuterastan made a few animals, birds, trees, and a hill. Then he sent Agocho, the Pigeon, to see how the world looked. Four days later Agocho returned and said all was beautiful, but that in four days more the water on the opposite side would rise and flood the land. Kuterastan at once created a pinon tree. This Stenatliha" skilfully tended until it grew to be of gigantic size at the end of four days. Then with four great Umbs as a framework she made a very large water bottle, tus, covering it with gum from the pinon. When the water appeared as predicted, Kuterastan went up on a cloud, taking his twenty-eight helpers with him, while Stenatliha summoned all the others and put them into the tus, into which she climbed last, closing the mouth at the top.

The flood completely submerged the earth for twelve days. Then the waters subsided, leaving the tus on the summit of the hill Kuterastan had made. The rush of the waters had changed the once smooth, level plain into series of mountains, hills, rivers, and valleys, so that Stenatliha hardly knew where they were when she opened the tus and came out. Tazhi, the Turkey, and Gage, the Crow, were the first to make a tour of the land. At the base of the hill they descended into a small muddy alkaline creek, in which the Turkey got the tips of his tail-feathers whitened, and they have been white ever since. On return they reported that all looked beautiful as far as they had travelled. Stenatliha then sent Agocho to make a complete circuit and let her know how things appeared on all sides. He came back much elated, for he had seen trees, grass, mountains, and beautiful lakes and rivers in every direction.

Directing the others to remain where she left them, Stenatliha summoned Hadintin Skhin, Hadintin Naln, Ndidilhldzn, and Agocho, and took them up in a cloud, in which they drifted until they met Kuterastan and his band of workers, who had completed the sky during the time of the flood. The two clouds floated to the top of the hill on which stood the tus. All descended to the valley below, where Stenatliha marshalled them into line, that Kuterastan might talk to them. He briefly told them that he was going to leave them and wished each one to do his part toward making the world perfect and happy. "You, Ndisagocha , shall have charge of the clouds and the water. You, Yadilhkih Skhin, I leave in charge of the sky. Nigostijn Nalin, you are to look after the crops of our people; and you, Hadintin Skhin, must care for their health and guide them." He then called Stenatliha to him and placed her in charge of all.

The people stood in line facing their god, with hands extended as if in supplication. Kuterastan and Stenatliha stood facing each other. Each rubbed their thighs with their hands, then cast their hands downward, and there arose between them a great pile of wood. Stenatliha knelt and slipped a hand under it, and as she did so Kuterastan passed his hand over the top. Great white billowy clouds of smoke at once issued forth, rising straight skyward. Into these Kuterastan disappeared. All the other gods and goddesses soon followed, leaving the twenty-eight whom Kuterastan had made to build the sky to remain upon the earth and people it. Chuganaai went east to travel with the sun; Stenatliha departed westward to make her home in clouds on the horizon, while Hadintin Skhin and Hadintin Nairn sought homes among the clouds in the south, and Nokuse may still be seen in the northern sky at night.

The Discovery of the Upper World (Jicarillas)

In the beginning all people, birds, and beasts were far beneath this earth, somewhere in the darkness; there was no sun, no moon. It was not a good place in which to live, because of the darkness. After a time came Chunnaai, the Sun, and Klenaai, the Moon. They directed the people to leave the world of darkness, showing the way they were to go by passing up through a rift in the sky. But the sky was so far above that the people knew of no way to reach it, so they made a pile of sand in the form of a mountain, and painted the east side white, the south blue, the west yellow, and the north side all colors. Then they gathered seeds from all the plants they knew and placed them inside the little mountain. Chunnaai sent back his messenger, Anltsistn, the Whirlwind, to instruct them how to make the mountain increase in size.

Then all gathered about it and danced and sang, until after four days the seeds sprouted and the mountain began to expand and to increase in height. This continued for four days, at the end of which time the mountain seemed almost to reach the sky; but suddenly its growth ceased, and none knew the cause. From Chunnaai came Whirlwind to tell the inhabitants how two of their maidens had entered the sacred space on the mountain top and had wantonly broken and destroyed plants and fruits, thus causing the mountain to cease growing.

With two long poles and four buffalo horns, which then were straight, the people made a ladder, which, when placed on the mountain top, reached the sky. One of the four Great Whirlwinds, Nichitso, went up to see what this new place was like. He put his head through the opening, and seeing that the world was covered with water, at once descended the ladder. The four Whirlwinds then went up; White Wind rolled the water to the east, but still there was water at the south; Blue Wind rolled it away to the south, but still there was water at the west; so Yellow Wind blew it away to the west, and then there was water only at the north, which All-Color Wind quickly blew away. Then the Winds blew over the earth for four days to dry it; but they left some of the water, which flowed along in streams.

When they returned and told what they had done, the people sent

X 1245-04

Kage, the Crow, who was wise, to view the land. They waited long, but Kage did not return. Then they sent Little Whirlwind, who found the Crow perched upon some dead bodies, plucking out their eyes; and because of his wickedness in forgetting the people, his feathers, once white, had turned black. Then Naga'schitn, the Badger, was sent to see if the land was good, but just as soon as he had crawled through he sank in the black mud and could go no farther, so Little Whirlwind was despatched to succor him. To this day Badger's legs are black. Next Keldishen, the Skunk, was sent, because he was light in weight; but even he sank in the mud and blackened his legs. Then the people sent Cha, the Beaver, who travelled about for a long time, and finding all the water running away in streams, built dams and thus formed many lakes. He came back and told the people that the land was good to live in, which pleased them greatly. Then they started up the ladder, and when all had passed over, it was found that their weight had bent the buffalo horns, which ever since have been curved. Thus all the people came out upon this earth at a place in the north.

During the first days the Sun did not rise above the horizon, having been held back in the east by a web that Masche, the Spider, had woven about him. But the people succeeded in tearing the web away, and from that time the Sun each day has travelled across the whole sky.

On emerging from the underworld the inhabitants began moving in a great circle, travelling from the north to the east, then to the south, then to the west. When any found a spot that pleased them, they settled there, and Chunnaai and Klenaai gave them a language of their own. Four times the land was thus encircled, but each time the circle became smaller, and when the people came the last time to the north, Haisndayin, the Jicarillas, found their home in the mountains near the Rio Chama.

Creation Myth (Navajo)

In the world below there was no sun and no moon, and therefore no light, yet vegetation in innumerable forms and the animal people thrived. Among the latter were Gray Wolf people, Naklétso; Mountain Lion, Nashtuítso; Badger, Naaschid; Locust, Woneschidi; Pine Squirrel, Klozeslskai and Klozeslzhlni; Blue Fox, Mai-Dotirshi; Yellow Fox, Mai-Iltsoi; Owl, Nascha; Crow, Gage; Buzzard, Jesho; four different varieties of the Hawk people, and many others.

Their world was small. At its eastern rim stood a large white mountain, and at the south a blue one. These formed the home of Astse Hastin, First Man. A yellow mountain in the west and a black one in the north harbored Astse Estsan, First Woman. Near the mountain in the east a large river had its source and flowed toward the south. Along its western bank the people lived in peace and plenty. There was game in abundance, much corn, and many edible fruits and nuts. All were happy. The younger women ground corn while the boys sang songs and played on flutes of the sunflower stalk. The men and the women had each eight chiefs, four living toward each cardinal point; the chiefs of the men lived in the east and south, those of the women in the west and north. The chiefs of the east took precedence over those of the south, as did those of the west over those of the north.

One day, led by their eight brave chiefs, all the men went off on a hunt. It occurred to the head-chief when they had been gone but a short time that the women should have been instructed to clean the camp thoroughly and bake a quantity of bread while all the men were away; so he despatched the youngest of the four chiefs of the south to the camp to make known his wishes, but instead of doing as bidden, the young chief visited with the head-chief's wife. The hunters were gone four days, at the end of which time they returned with much game, weary and very hungry. To their surprise they found the camp in a very unkempt condition and no bread baked in anticipation of their return. The messenger was called before the head-chief at once and questioned as to the directions he had given the women. He explained that he had told the chief of the women what they were expected to do, but she refused to listen to him, and he

was powerless to do more. Then the head-chief went to his wife and demanded to know why she had refused to issue his orders to the women. She curtly replied that that was her business and not his; as it was, the women did more work than the men, for they tilled the fields, made the clothing, cared for the children, and did the cooking, while the men did practically nothing, so if they chose to spend a few days in idleness, it was nothing more than they had a right to do and no one's concern but their own. The chief became angry, and during a quarrel that ensued he was told that he and all his followers might leave if they would, for the women could get along better without them.

Remonstrance and reasoning availed nothing; the chief of the women grew more vehement as she argued, so the head-chief determined to put the women to the test. The following morning he issued orders that all the men in camp prepare to depart, for the women had declared they could live better independently of them and were to be given an opportunity to do so.

Having decided to cross the great river flowing from the east, work at once began on four large cottonwood rafts to be used as ferries. Four days it took to put all in readiness, and at dawn of the fifth day the crossing of the stream began. Orders were issued that all food supplies, clothing, and utensils be left with the women, save enough seed corn to plant crops the next spring, and no males, infant or aged, were to be left behind. Four nutli (hermaphrodites) objected strongly at being taken from the women, but were forced to join the men, as they were needed to care for the babies. Four old cripples, too weak to move, were left behind, but other than these not a male inhabitant remained in the old village at the end of four days. After all had crossed the river, the rafts were fastened securely to the bank in order that the women might not get them and follow.

As soon as the men had landed they began to work with zeal, for houses had to be built, game caught, skins tanned, and land prepared for crops. They suffered much from scarcity of food and clothing the first winter, but managed to exist. The women, however, had bountiful crops, and all through the late fall and winter could be heard revelling in great delight, feasting daily and dancing much of the time to the music of songs sung by the four old cripples. The following autumn found the men in much better circumstances, for they had grown small crops; but the women were less fortunate. Having none but themselves to work and provide for, they had become negligent from the beginning, dissipating the contents of their granaries and allowing their fields to grow fallow. By the end of the second year clothing had become very scarce, and not knowing how to hunt, they had no way to obtain more skins. The men, on the contrary, had grown more prosperous; their well-tended farms yielded an ample supply of corn for the winter, and the pelts of deer and antelope furnished a deal of warm clothing and bedding. The third year found the men living in ease and comfort, while the women had become reduced to absolute want, many having fallen ill from self-neglect. They called across to the men, pleading to be taken over and promising faithful allegiance, but the chief was resolute and refused to forget how he had been wronged.

Then it was that the youngest of the eight ruling men, in a moment of compassion, confessed his guilt, admitting in a plea to the head-chief for clemency that he was in fact responsible for the attitude his wife had taken. This served only to renew the old chief's anger; he stoutly refused to listen to further appeals and expressed his regret that the first seeds of wrong should have been thus sown. No longer able to keep up the fight, with starvation staring them in the face, and being in nakedness, at the end of the fourth year the women attempted to swim the river in parties, but the attempts resulted only in death, for the swift current would have been too much even for the strongest men to buffet. Seeing this self-sacrifice and realizing that the race would be ultimately exterminated if the women continued it much longer, appeals were made daily to the head-chief to permit the rescue of the remainder. Four times was he sought to grant such permission before he consented, then at dawn of the fifth morning he gave directions to loose the rafts and ferry the women over. A miserable remnant they were, unclad, wan, and wasted; but a return to the old habits of life soon restored them to their former selves, and peace, happiness, and prosperity reigned again.

The broad river that flowed from the east had its source in two very large springs, a he-spring and a she-spring, in which lived two large Water Monsters. These had a pair of youngsters who delighted in emerging from the depths of the spring and swimming out across the meadows in the shallow water where there was neither current nor river banks. Coyote spied them one day, and being ever a meddler and trouble-maker –though withal a fellow of polished mien—stole them, putting the two under the folds of his jacket.

Now there was no sun, moon, or stars to give light; but in the east every morning appeared White Dawn four fingers high. The midday was lighted by Blue Dawn in the south, and late afternoon by Yellow Dawn from the west. The north remained always dark. On the morning following Coyote's return from his trip to the east, ostensibly to discover, if possible, the source of the dawn, the head-chief noticed that it was not so broad as usual—only three fingers high, with a dark streak beneath. A Wolf man was sent to learn what was wrong. He hurried off, returning at nightfall with the report that all was well in the east. The next morning White Dawn was much narrower and the darkness beneath had increased. A Mountain Lion messenger was despatched to seek the cause. He reported everything in normal condition, but those in camp noticed deer

X1078-04

in the distance travelling westward at a rapid pace. The third morning the belt of darkness was wider than White Dawn, which now gave an alarmingly dim light. The chief then sent White Hawk to investigate the trouble, under orders of haste. His report, like that of each of the other messengers, was that nothing unusual appeared in the east. More deer, antelope, and other game animals, however, were seen running westward in apparent fright.

On the fourth morning White Dawn was entirely obscured; nothing but darkness appeared in the east. Sparrow-hawk sped away, returning in a very brief time with the report that water was fast rising in the two springs at the head of the river and might soon spread westward in a great devastating wave. Instantly the camp became a scene of commotion. Quickly gathering together what corn and other seeds they could carry, the people started in haste for the White Mountain in the east. On reaching the top they saw the waters climbing rapidly up the eastern slope, so they descended and ran to the Blue Mountain in the south, taking with them handfuls of earth from its crest, and from its base a reed with twelve sections, which a Wolf man carried.

From the top of the Blue Mountain it was seen that the wave of water, fast approaching, would submerge them, so snatching handfuls of earth from it they hurried on to the Yellow Mountain in the west. The oncoming wave seemed higher than ever, so again they ran on, this time toward the north, where the Black Mountain stood, taking as before handfuls of earth and another reed, entrusted to Mountain Lion. Here the water surrounded them and slowly crept up the sides of the mountain. The female reed from the west was planted on the western side near the top, the male reed from the east on the eastern slope, and both at once began to shoot upward rapidly. Into the twelve internodes of the female reed climbed all the women, while the men made haste to get into theirs. Turkey being the last to get in, the foamy waters caught his tail, whitening the tips of the feathers, which are so to this day.

The reeds grew very rapidly, but equally fast rose the waters around them. Four days the reeds grew thus, at the end of the fourth day meeting at the sky. This seemed an impenetrable banker for a time, but Locust had taken with him his bow of darkness and sacred arrows. With these he made a hole in the sky and passed on into the world above—the present earth.

The earth was small, devoid of vegetation of any kind, and covered in greater part by water in which lived four Monsters with great blue horns. These had their homes at the cardinal points, and just as soon as Locust made his appearance arrows came whizzing at him from all quarters. Failing to harm him with their arrows, which he dodged with ease, the Monsters bade him leave at once, threatening immediate death

if he tarried; adding that visitors were not desired and were always destroyed at sight.

Locust replied that he intended no harm, but would insist upon remaining with them for a time, for he had many followers for whom he was seeking a home. Seeing that Locust had no fear of them and had proved too agile to be hit with arrows, the Monsters sought to kill him by trickery. Each took two heavy arrows, swallowed them, and pulled them out through their flanks, saying, "Do this and you may remain." Locust followed their example, escaping unharmed.

"Now," said he, "I did your trick, let me ask you to do one of mine." Then taking four sacred arrows he passed them transversely through his chest, back and forth, one at a time. As he pulled each arrow out the second time he passed it to one of the four Monsters, saying, "If you can do this, my people will not come; if not, then I shall send for them and we shall all make this our home." Each placed an arrow to his chest and pushed, but cringed with pain as soon as it penetrated the skin. Fearing the Monsters might not proceed. Locust quickly blew toward each of the arrows, which shot through their bodies, instantly killing them. In the east now flows Red river, made red by the blood of these Monsters; and holes yet remain through the thorax of the locust.

Impatient at the delay in Locust's return. Badger climbed through the hole in the sky and followed the tracks to where Locust had been in controversy with the slain Monsters. Seeing their bodies lying out in the shallow water, he thought he would go over and inspect them, but he sank into the soft black mud, which made him retreat. The mud blackened his legs, which have remained the same to this day.

With a large stone knife Locust cut off the horns of the Monsters one by one. With those from the one toward the east he made a long sweep with his arm in that direction, and in the distance sprang up an ocean. In like manner he formed oceans to the south, west, and north with the horns of the remaining three. The creation of rivers followed: with a wave of the hand the Rio Grande, the San Juan, the Colorado, the Little Colorado, and others were made. Hair pulled from the bodies of the Monsters was tossed to the winds and from it sprang frogs, snakes, lizards, and reptiles of every kind.

While Locust was doing this the remainder of the people came up. They stood about on the small bare spots of ground wondering what to do. Among them were the four Winds (Nilchi), Black, Blue, Yellow, and White. Each blew toward his respective cardinal point and soon much of the water dried up, leaving a quantity of bare land. But not a sign of vegetation was there at any hand; all was as barren as the desert sands. Luckily each had brought seeds of many kinds from the world below. These they began planting, finishing the task in four days.

XI064-04

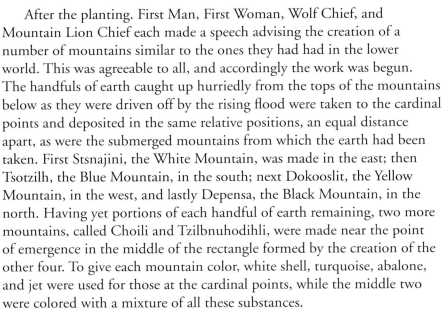

Creation Myth (Navajo)

After the planting. First Man, First Woman, Wolf Chief, and Mountain Lion Chief each made a speech advising the creation of a number of mountains similar to the ones they had had in the lower world. This was agreeable to all, and accordingly the work was begun. The handfuls of earth caught up hurriedly from the tops of the mountains below as they were driven off by the rising flood were taken to the cardinal points and deposited in the same relative positions, an equal distance apart, as were the submerged mountains from which the earth had been taken. First Stsnajini, the White Mountain, was made in the east; then Tsotzilh, the Blue Mountain, in the south; next Dokooslit, the Yellow Mountain, in the west, and lastly Depensa, the Black Mountain, in the north. Having yet portions of each handful of earth remaining, two more mountains, called Choili and Tzilbnuhodihli, were made near the point of emergence in the middle of the rectangle formed by the creation of the other four. To give each mountain color, white shell, turquoise, abalone, and jet were used for those at the cardinal points, while the middle two were colored with a mixture of all these substances.

When the mountains were finished and the people looked about, it was proposed that a sky should be made to cover the earth. "But," said one, "what of the earth itself; is it not too small to furnish food for the people who shall later come to live upon it?" None had thought of this, but reflection, followed by a discussion, brought them all to the one opinion—they would enlarge the earth and at the same time spread the sky above. Accordingly, the chief who had spoken asked if anyone had a piece of turquoise weighing as much as a man, and the skin of a large male deer which had been smothered to death in pollen. First Man answered that he had. A large white shell and the skin of a doe which had been smothered in pollen were next requested. First Woman responded with them. The two skins were then placed on the ground, side by side, with their heads toward the east. Upon the one was put the turquoise and a piece of abalone shell; on the other the white shell and a pearl. First Man and First Woman then called for Kosdilhkih, Black Cloud, and Adilhkih, Black Fog. These came and spread out over the skins four times each, lifting and settling each time. When Fog lifted the last time it took up with it the skin with the turquoise and abalone and began to expand, spreading wider and wider until a blue film covered all, in the form of the sky. As the turquoise skin expanded, so also did the white-shell skin, broadening the earth as it grew. During this period of transition the people all travelled eastward, and being Holy People, covered great distances each day. At the end of the fourth day they stopped. Then also the sky and the earth ceased widening, having reached their present dimensions. Since the two skins had been placed with their heads toward the east, the heads of the sky and the earth are now in that direction.

As yet there was neither sun nor moon to shed light, only dawn, circling the horizon in the four colors: white in the east, blue in the south, yellow in the west, and black in the north. Deeming it necessary that they should have light to brighten the world, and warmth for the com and the grass, on their return to the earth's centre one of the chiefs made a speech advocating the creation of a sun and a moon.

First Man and First Woman placed two sacred deerskins on the ground as before. On the buckskin a shell of abalone was placed, on the doeskin a bowl made of pearl. The shell contained a piece of clear quartz crystal, and the bowl a moss agate. The objects were dressed respectively in garments of white, blue, yellow, and black wind, and were carried to the end of the land in the east by First Man and First Woman. With their spirit power Astse Hastin and Astse Estsan sent both the shell and the bowl far out over the ocean, giving life to the crystal and the agate as they did so, directing that the one who would be known as Chehonaai, the Sun, should journey homeward through the sky by day, shedding light and warmth as he passed; the other, Klehonaai, the Moon, must travel the same course by night. To each were given homes of turquoise in the east and west, and none but the Winds and the gods, Haschelti and Haschogan, were to visit them.

Upon their return Astse Hastin and Astse Estsan were asked if they would leave the sky in so plain a condition, or if they intended to beautify it with jewels. They replied that it was their intention to dot it with many bright stars. All those who had bits of white shell, turquoise, crystal, pearl, or abalone were directed to contribute them for the making of the stars. These were placed upon the two deerskins by First Man and First Woman. The seven stars of the Great Dipper, Nohokos Bakun, were the first to be set in the sky. Next, those of Nohokos Baad, his female complement, were placed in the blue dome. Then followed Etetso and Etetsozi, Sontso and Sontsozi, and Dilgehet, the Small Dipper, Sonhotsi and Klekai Stai, the Milky Way.

In each instance the arrangement of the stars in the constellation was made when the fragments of precious stones were placed upon the skins, where Astse Hastin and Astse Estsan imparted glowing light to them and delivered them to the Winds to carry to the sky. Only a small portion of the gems had been thus transformed and sent up, when a fine-looking, well-dressed stranger came up to watch the proceedings. In reply to his question as to what was being done, his attention was directed to the sun, the moon, and the many stars already created, while more were soon to follow. The man was Coyote, son of Darkness.

He watched the work for a time, when, seeing his chance, he caught the large deerskin containing the pile of jewel fragments and flung it skyward, blowing into the bits four times ere they could fall, scattering

them all over the sky. Thus it is that there are myriads of stars irregular in arrangement and without names. As he strode off Coyote explained curtly that there were already enough sacred things to worship.

Then the Winds were stationed at the horizon to guard the earth, and at the four sacred mountains in the east, south, west,and north, to act as messengers for the Haschelti and Haschogan—Talking Gods and House Gods—who had their abodes on them. On the same plane, one behind the other, the Winds were ranged in streaks. White, Blue, Yellow, and Black. Outside of all Coyote placed a streak of Red Wind. This forced itself to the inside many years later and gave rise to disease and premature death, for as the good Winds are life-breathing, so the evil Winds are life-taking. Even now the Red Wind takes the lives of many children every year.

The Digln made their homes near Choili, close to the place of emergence. It was there that all ceremonies took place. From their homes the people saw a dark Cloud settle and cover the top of Choili. For four days it kept lowering until the mountain was completely shrouded in dark blue fog. They did not know whether it portended good or evil, but realized that something of moment was at hand. Astse Hastin ascended the mountain through the fog to learn what it meant, but found nothing unusual. As he turned to descend, a faint, apparently distant cry reached his ears, but he paid no heed. Ere long the same sound came to him again; then a third and a fourth time, whereupon he turned and walked in the direction whence it came. On the eastern slope he found a tiny baby, and wrapping it in rays of sunbeams he carried it home to his wife.

The Cloud that descended was a portion of the sky which had come to meet the Earth; from the union of the two Yolkai Estsan, White-Shell Woman, was born. In twelve days the baby had grown to maturity, subsisting on pollen only. Astse Hastin and Astse Estsan sent messengers to all the Digin to tell them of the marvel and to summon them to a ceremony which would be held four days later. Word was sent also to the gods on the four sacred mountains.

Astse Estsan dressed Yolkai Estsan in fine garments ornamented with beautiful jewels. At the western side of her hogan she placed a sacred deerskin and laid upon it several wool and cotton blankets, covering the whole with a mountain-lion skin. These were arranged as the seat of honor for White-Shell Woman, for whom was about to be held a ceremony celebrating her maturity.

On the appointed day all assembled. The first matter to decide was the number of songs to be sung. Some wished fourteen, others thought twelve sufficient. Haschelti, Talking God, sang the songs and chose to sing fourteen. When he had finished, each of the Holy People sang six songs, making in all two hundred and eighty-two. An entire night

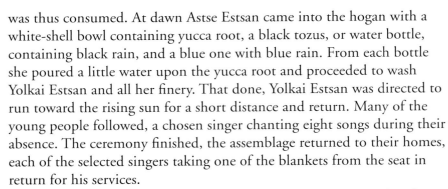

was thus consumed. At dawn Astse Estsan came into the hogan with a white-shell bowl containing yucca root, a black tozus, or water bottle, containing black rain, and a blue one with blue rain. From each bottle she poured a little water upon the yucca root and proceeded to wash Yolkai Estsan and all her finery. That done, Yolkai Estsan was directed to run toward the rising sun for a short distance and return. Many of the young people followed, a chosen singer chanting eight songs during their absence. The ceremony finished, the assemblage returned to their homes, each of the selected singers taking one of the blankets from the seat in return for his services.

Although all the people then on earth were of the Digin, only a few had god-like powers, particularly First Man, First Woman, Yolkai Estsan, and the Winds. The lesser Holy Ones worked much in clay, making pottery and adobe houses. The designs they used in their earthenware, however, were of a sacred nature, to be used only in ceremonials, and when the Fox, Wolf, Badger, Bird, and many other people repeatedly employed sacred symbols to adorn their cooking pots. First Man and his wife became very angry and called a council, which, in addition to themselves, was attended by Chehonaai, Yolkai Estsan, and Nilchi, the Wind People.

The wicked people had homes throughout the land, many of which were built of stone, upon the plains, and others in the cliffs. The councillors decided that these people and their homes must be destroyed, but how to effect this was a problem.

First Woman and Chehonaai thought it would be wise to give birth to demoniac monsters and let them devour the evil ones, but First Man objected, and finally the council agreed that the Winds should perform the task by bringing forth a devastating storm. The faithful were warned and given time to seek refuge under the water, inside the sacred mountains, in the higher cliffs, and in the sky. Then the Winds came. For four days terrific storms raged, hurling men and trees and houses through the air like leaves. When they abated hundreds of houses lay in ruins which may yet be traced by heaps of stones scattered throughout the Navaho country.

Soon another council of the same dictators was called, this time to discuss how more people might be created. First Man sent Wind messengers to bring Black Fog Boy and Black Cloud Girl, Precious Stone Boy and Precious Stone Girl, White Corn Boy and Yellow Corn Girl, Blue Corn Boy and All-Color Corn Girl, Pollen Boy and Cricket Girl, and Rain Boy and Rain Girl. These twelve were laid side by side on four sacred deerskins and covered with four others. The Spirit Winds of the west came and blew between the skins; the Spirit Winds of the east came and blew also; then came Haschelti from the east, with rainbows in his hand, calling "Wu-hu-hu-hu-u"; and Haschogan from the south, with sunbeams in his hand. They walked up and gently tapped the skins with their bows and beams. Haschelti of the west and Haschogan of the north came next and gently tapped the skins. Then the skins lifted, revealing twelve beautiful young people perfectly formed. Astse Hastin bade them arise and stand, and then with Haschelti in the lead and Haschogan behind, they four times encircled the sacred mountains Choili and Tzilhnuhodihir, halting close to the hole whence the Holy People emerged. There Astse Hastin made them an extended speech, telling them that they had been brought forth from the elements to people the earth; that they must rear children and care for them as kind fathers and mothers, teaching them to be good to one another; and that it would be necessary for them to plant corn and other seeds at once. The Digin, First Man continued, were about to leave, to go into the rivers, the oceans, the cliffs, the mountains, off to the horizon, and to the sky, but they would ever keep watch over their people and would help those who showed them respect and reverence in prayer and song. To Yolkai Estsan was entrusted future guardianship of the people. It would be her duty to furnish the he-rain and the she-rain, to fructify all crops, and bring forth abundant grass and seeds.

Then the Digin took their departure, vanishing the people knew not whither. Yolkai Estsan turned westward to her white shell home on the horizon, far out across the wide waters. Arriving there she determined to make a few more people. Cuticle rubbed from her body, with bits of white shell, turquoise, abalone, and jet, she placed between two sacred deerskins, male and female, and called for the Spirit Winds of the east, the Spirit Winds of the west, Haschelti and Haschogan, who came and breathed upon and tapped the deerskins as once before, and lo! there arose four pairs of people.

Each pair was given a walking-stick—one of white shell to one, staffs of turquoise, abalone, and jet respectively to the others. Black Fog and Black Cloud came and spread out over the water. Upon these the new people took up their journey eastward to join others like themselves. For four days they travelled on Fog and Cloud, reaching the earth at the end of the fourth day, where, on the following day, they were welcomed by Chehonaai, the Sun. There, too, the Bear, the Wolf, the Great Snake, the Mountain Lion, the Weasel, and the Porcupine met them at the direction of Yolkai Estsan, to guard them on their long land journey. The Lightning also she made, to protect them from above.

They journeyed eastward, stopping to camp and rest at the end of the first day. For water they had but to prod the earth with their walking-sticks and a spring gushed forth. The first of the four, the man of White Shell, stuck his staff into the ground and water came up at once. "The water is close," he remarked, from which speech he took his name, for the others henceforth called him To Ahani, Water Is Close. The following

Creation Myth (Navajo)

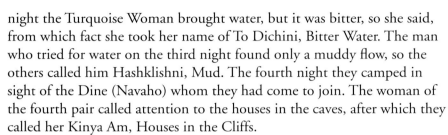

night the Turquoise Woman brought water, but it was bitter, so she said, from which fact she took her name of To Dichini, Bitter Water. The man who tried for water on the third night found only a muddy flow, so the others called him Hashklishni, Mud. The fourth night they camped in sight of the Dine (Navaho) whom they had come to join. The woman of the fourth pair called attention to the houses in the caves, after which they called her Kinya Am, Houses in the Cliffs.

The following day they were welcomed by the twelve who had been created and given dominion over the land but a short time before, and from these twenty have the pure-blood Navaho descended.

The Bird of Ages (Cree)

The waters were spread over the face of the earth; there was nothing to be seen but one vast and entire ocean, save the mighty Bird of Ages, which had lived from the beginning of time, whose eyes were fire, whose glances were lightning, and the clapping of whose wings was thunder. He had lived long in the skies above the stars; but, when he heard the rushing and dashing about of the waters, he descended from his seat to the ocean, and touching it, the earth instantly rose, and remained on the surface of the water. It rose of its present size, covered with verdure, as the low grounds which have been flooded by winter rains are green when these rains are withdrawn from them. The mountains, then as now, towered to the skies, and the valleys were deep, and the rivers rushed impetuously over the steeps which attempted to impede their course. Winters locked up a portion of the earth, and the summer suns beamed fiercely and intensely upon another portion. The stars shone by day, and the beams of the moon gladdened the hours of darkness. Winds swept the vast expanse of ocean, and a part of the time was calm as a part of the time is now. The world was very like what it is at this day, save that, within its mighty boundaries, over all its far limits, neither on mountain, hill, valley, tree, nor bush, in den nor burrow, in water nor air, dwelt a living creature. No gentle song of bird arose to break the stillness of morning, no cry of wild beast to disturb the unbroken hush of midnight; the noise of the winds chasing each other over the vast waste was all that was heard breaking the monotonous repose of the earth.

"This will not do," said the Bird, talking to himself; "here is a fine world and nobody to occupy it. Here are stars, beautiful as anything can be; a moon, that sheds her mild light on—what?—and a sun so bright that not even the Bird of Ages can look steadily on his beams—with that bird alone to behold him or them. How balmy is the air which I feel fanning my feathers!—but it cannot breathe to revive the human heart after sickness or toil, or gladden the spirit of the beast which lies panting in the shade from excessive heat. It is lost, wasted, and so are the beams of the sun, the moon, and the stars; and so are the sweet fruits that grow spontaneously about the earth, and the beautiful flowers that waste their

fragrance on the desert air. This must not be," repeated the Bird.

So he flew up to the highest pinnacle of the Mountain of the Thunders, and there fell to musing, the while scratching the side of his head with his mighty claw. At last he bethought himself of a spell or charm, which was taught him by his father, who lived before time was, and survived its commencement many ages. He recollected that this venerable and wise bird, who did not die till his claws were rotted off, and his feathers all dispersed to the winds, told him that if one of his descendants were to eat nothing for seven days, and to quench his thirst with the dew which should lie upon the mountain-laurel, he would enjoy the power to accomplish that which ought to be done. "Nothing can be clearer," said the Bird of Ages to himself, "than that the world ought to be inhabited. Now I, by fasting seven days, and quenching my thirst with the dew of the mountain-laurel alone, shall, according to the word of my father, be enabled to see this earth tenanted by beautiful creatures; the seeds, which now lie dormant in the earth, will spring up to furnish food for innumerable creatures, and those innumerable creatures will enjoy the bounties spread out in such profusion before them! How delightful it will be to see and hear the birds of soft notes and splendid plumage, singing and hopping about on bush and tree; and the kid, and the fawn, and the lamb, gambolling on the sunny hill-side, and the fishes disporting in their own element; and Man, the lord of all, painted on his cheek and brow with the ochre of wrath, and wearing the gallant scalp-lock, decked with the plumes of the eagle; and to hear his cry of battle, rising from the gathering place of warriors, and to mark the pole of red scalps, and better yet the resolution of the captive, when the torments are inflicted upon him, when the pincers tear his flesh, when the hot stones sear his eyeballs. All these pleasures will delight the eyes and ears of those who shall live on this beautiful world, when I shall have done what I conceive ought to have been done."

So he commenced his fast. Seven days he ate no food, and quenched his thirst with only the dew which lay upon the mountain-laurel. Upon the morning of the eighth day he began his task. "There ought to be a vast number of fishes," said he, "and of different sizes, for each must feed upon the other and smaller." So he called into existence all the fishes that people the waters. Then he said to the quadrupeds and four-footed beasts, to worms and snakes, and every thing else which are not fishes, "Be, for you ought to be;" and they were. So the earth became peopled and inhabited. All were called into existence then, and in that manner, except the Chepewyans, and they had their origin ages after, from the loins of a dog; which was performed thus:

There was among the Crees a man, whose upper lip was split, displaying the upper teeth to every one that saw him; he was not a

courageous man, but feared every thing in the shape of danger; even the cry of beasts and the singing of birds, and the growl of the bear, and the song of the bittern, alarmed him. He was very fond of dogs, and possessed the power of transforming them into the shape of men, though he was without the power to make them continue in that shape for a longer period than that between sun and sun. He could make a wolf-dog step into the form of a handsome hunter; he could clothe an old cur with the skin of a very wise *powwow*. After his charm was spoken over a spaniel sneaking with his tail between his legs, you would see, in his stead, a white man doing the very same mean act of cowardice, with his back upon his enemy. A hoity-toity little she-puppy would become in a twinkling a very pretty girl; and an ugly old snarling she-wolf, a crabbed and sour old squaw. But, when the sun arose, the handsome hunter became again the wolf-dog; and the very wise *powwow*, the old cur; and the white man running from his enemy, the spaniel sneaking off with his tail between his legs; and the very pretty girl, the hoity-toity little she-puppy; and the crabbed and sour old squaw, the ugly and snarling old she wolf-dog. He would have been very glad to have made them retain the form of human beings, but he possessed not the power. At last, he bethought himself of the mighty Bird of Ages, who dwelt among the lofty peaks of the Mountain of Thunders. To this bird he repaired, and telling him what he had come for, he received the command to go to the Lake of the Woods, and bring thence a flat, white stone, which lay upon the southern shore of that lake. It possessed, the mighty Bird said, the power to enable almost any thing to be done which should be asked of it by men of the Cree nation; by the great ancestor of which it had been endued with its present power.

The man did as he was bidden. He went to the southern shore of the Lake of the Woods, and brought away the great white *memahoppa*, or medicine-stone, which has ever since remained with the Crees. Having placed this stone in the corner of his cabin, and addressed it as his tutelar deity, he proceeded to make the transformation of a fine, handsome, courageous, young dog into the shape of a man. When this was effected, he led the man to the *memahoppa*, and first praying the sacred stone to protect him against the power of change, he placed the man upon it. The charm was effective. The wonderful properties of the medicine-stone operated to keep the man a man. And this man married a woman of the Crees, and from them are the Chepewyans descended.

When the mighty Bird of Ages had finished his work of calling into existence the different creatures, he made a great arrow to be the sign of the deeds he had done; with the command that it should remain lodged in the great council-house of the Chepewyans, until time should be no more. As long as they should obey this command, they should ever be victorious

over their enemies, and fortunate in all their hunting expeditions; their word should be law to all the tribes and nations, from the Frozen Sea to the land of the Shawanos, from the towns of the Iroquois to the Mountains of Thunder. But, whenever they should by carelessness lose it, they should be doomed to encounter their full share of the losses and defeats, and difficulties, and disappointments, which belong to other and less favoured tribes. They should sometimes be overcome by a force of inferior numbers; and often seek the beasts of the chace for many weary days without finding them. And, saying thus, he gave the arrow into the hands of the chief man of the Chepewyans.

For many, very many ages, the Chepewyans scrupulously remembered the injunctions of the mighty Bird respecting the arrow, and kept it treasured up in the house of the great council. While they did so, they were the most fortunate tribe on the earth, and became lords over all, conquerors in every battle, and the most fortunate hunters the world has ever known. But, at length carelessness got the better of prudence, and they suffered the arrow to be stolen; the sacrilege so enraged the Bird of Ages, that he quitted the earth, and winged his way to the place he inhabited before he descended from above. He has never been seen on earth since; but the Chepewyans, and other tribes whom this tale has reached, believe that the thunder of the hot moons is the clapping of his wings, and the lightning which accompanies it, the glancing of his eye. When a dark cloud that has no rain crosses the earth, they say he is flying between it and the sun; and they believe that the snow of the winter is the down which he strips from his breast.

Alaskan Creation Myths (Inuit)

Origin of the Land and the People (Inuit)

In the beginning there was water over all the earth. There were no people. It was very cold. The water was covered with ice, and the ice pieces ground together, making long ridges and hummocks.

Then a man came from the other side of the great water and stopped on the ice hills. He took for his wife a wolf. Then their children grew up. Each pair spoke a different language from that of their parents, or from that of their brothers and sisters. So each pair went out in a different direction and built houses on the ice hills. Then the snow melted and ran down the hill-sides. It scooped out ravines and river beds and made the earth. Thus the earth was made and the people. That is why so many different languages are spoken.

Creation of the World (Athapascan)

A long time ago, water flowed all over the world. There was one family and they made a big raft. Then they put animals on the raft Now there was no land but all water, so the people wanted to make a world. The man tied a cord around a beaver and sent him down to find the bottom of the water. But the beaver got only half-way and drowned. Then the man tied a string around a muskrat and sent him down. Muskrat drowned, but he reached the bottom and got a little mud on his hands. Then the man took the mud out of the muskrat's hands into his palm. He let it dry and then crumbled it to dust. Then he blew the dust out of his palm all over the waters. This made the world.

Origin of Mankind (Inuit)

Long, long ago, a man and a woman came down from the sky and landed on one of the Diomede Islands. They lived there a long while, but they had no children. At last one day the man took some walrus ivory, and from this he carved five dolls, just like people. Then he took some wood and made from it five more dolls. Then, one night, when all were finished,

MADONNA OF THE NORTH

COPYRIGHT 1913

H G Kaiser

NOME ALASKA

he set them off to one side, all ten in a row. The next morning the dolls had become people. The ivory dolls became men, therefore they are brave and hardy; but the wooden dolls became women, therefore they are soft and timid. From these ten dolls came all the people of the Diomede Islands.

The Origin of Fire (Tlingit)

Long ago, in the days of the animal people, Raven saw a fire far out at sea. He tied a piece of pitch to Chicken Hawk's bill. He said, "Go out to the fire, touch it with the pitchwood, and bring it back." Chicken Hawk did so. The fire stuck to the pitchwood and he brought it back to Raven. Then Raven put the fire into the rock and into the red cedar. Then he said, "Thus shall you get your fire—from this rock and from this red cedar." The tribes did as he told them.

The Origin of the Winds (Tlingit)

Now Raven went off to a certain place and created West Wind. Raven said to it, "You shall be my son's daughter. No matter how hard you blow, you shall hurt nobody."

Raven also made South Wind. When South Wind climbs on top of a rock it never ceases to blow.

Raven made North Wind and on top of a mountain he made a house for it with ice hanging down the sides. Then he went in and said to North Wind, "Your back is white." That is why mountains are white with snow.

The First Woman (Inuit)

Long, long ago there were many men living in the northland, but there was no woman among them. Far away in the southland lived one woman. At last one of the young men in the northland travelled south to the home of the woman and married her. He thought, "I have a wife, while the son of the headsman has none."

Now the son of the headsman had also started to travel to the home of the woman in the southland. He stood in the passage to the house and heard the husband talking to himself. So he waited until all the people were asleep. Then the son of the headsman crept into the house and began to drag the woman away. He caught her by her shoulders.

Then the husband was awakened. He ran to the passage and caught the woman by her feet. So the men pulled until they pulled the woman in two. The son of the headsman carried the upper part of her body to the north. Then they began to carve wood to make each woman complete.

Thus there were now two women.

The woman in the south was a good dancer; but she could not do fine needlework in sewing the furs, because her hands were wooden. The woman in the north was a poor dancer, because her feet were wooden, but she could sew with fine stitches in the furs. So all the women of the north are skilful with their hands, and all the women of the south are good dancers, even to this day. Thus you may know that the tale is true.

The Bringing of the Light by Raven (Inuit)

In the first days, the sun and moon were in the sky. Then the sun and moon were taken away and people had only the light of the stars. Even the magic of the shamans failed to bring back the light.

Now there was an orphan boy in the village who sat with the humble people over the entrance way of the kashim. He was despised by every one. When the magic of the shamans failed to bring back the sun and moon into the sky the boy mocked them. He said, "What fine shamans you must be. You cannot bring back the light, but I can." Then the shamans were angry and beat that boy and drove him out of the kashim. Now this boy was like any other boy until he put on a raven coat he had. Then he became Raven.

Now the boy went to his aunt's house. He told her the shamans had failed to bring back the light, and they had beaten him when he mocked them. The boy said, "Where are the sun and moon?"

The aunt said, "I do not know."

The boy said, "I am sure you know. Look what a finely sewed coat you wear. You could not sew it that way if you did not know where the light is."

Thus they argued.

Then the aunt said, "If you wish to find the light, go far to the south. Go on snowshoes. You will know the place when you get there."

The boy put on his snowshoes and set off toward the south. Many days he travelled and the darkness was always the same. When he had gone a very long way he saw far in front of him a ray of light. Then the boy hurried on. As he went farther the light showed again, plainer than before. Then it vanished for a time. Thus it kept appearing and vanishing.

At last the boy came to a large hill. One side was brightly lighted; the other side was black as night. Close to the hill was a hut. A man was shovelling snow from in front of it. The man tossed the snow high in the air; then the light could not be seen until the snow fell. Then the man tossed the snow again. So the light kept appearing and disappearing. Close to the house was a large ball of fire.

The Bringing of the Light by Raven (Inuit)

The boy stopped and began to plan how to steal the ball of light.

Then the boy walked up to the man. He said, "Why do you throw up the snow? It hides the light from our village."

The man said, "I am not hiding the light. I am clearing away the snow. Who are you? Where did you come from?"

The boy said, " It is so dark at our village I do not want to stay there. I came here to live with you."

"All the time?" asked the man.

"Yes," said the boy.

The man said, "All right. Come into the house with me." Then he dropped his shovel on the ground. He stooped down to lead the way through the underground passage into the house. He let the curtain fall in front of the door as he passed, because he thought the boy was close beside him.

Then the boy caught up the ball of light. He put it in the turned-up flap of his fur coat. Then he picked up the shovel and ran away toward the north. He ran until his feet were tired. Then he put on his raven coat and flew away. He flew rapidly to the north. Raven could hear the man shriek behind him. The man was pursuing him. But Raven flew faster. Then the man cried, "Keep the light; but give me my shovel."

Raven said, "No, you cannot have your shovel. You made our village dark." So Raven flew faster.

Now as Raven flew, he broke off a little piece of the light. This made day. Then he went on a long time in darkness, until he broke off another piece of light.

Thus it was day again. So as Raven flew to the village he broke off the pieces of light. When Raven reached the kashim of his own village he threw away the last piece. He went into the kashim and said to the shamans, "I have brought back the light. It will be light and then dark, so as to make day and night."

After this Raven went out upon the ice because his home was on the seacoast. Then a great wind arose, and the ice drifted with him across the sea to the land on the other side.

Thus Raven brought back the light. It is night and day, as he said it would be. But sometimes the nights are very long because Raven travelled a long way without throwing away a piece of the light.

The First Totem Pole (Kwakiutl)

Once there was a chief who had never had a dance. All the other chiefs had big dances, but Wakiash none. Therefore Wakiash was unhappy. He thought for a long while about the dance. Then he went up into the mountains to fast. Four days he fasted. On the fourth day he fell asleep. Then something fell on his breast. It was a green frog. Frog said, "Wake up." Then Wakiash waked up. He looked about to see where he was. Frog said, "You are on Raven's back. Raven will fly around the world with you."

So Raven flew. Raven flew all around the world. Raven showed Wakiash everything in the world. On the fourth day, Raven flew past a house with a totem pole in front of it. Wakiash could hear singing in the house. Wakiash wished he could take the totem pole and the house with him. Now Frog knew what Wakiash was thinking. Frog told Raven. Raven stopped and Frog told Wakiash to hide behind the door. Frog said, "When they dance, jump out into the room."

The people in the house began to dance. They were animal people. But they could not sing or dance. One said, "Something is the matter. Someone is near us."

Chief said, "Let one who can run faster than the flames go around the house and see."

So Mouse went. Mouse could go anywhere, even into a box. Now Mouse looked like a woman; she had taken off her animal clothes. Mouse ran out, but Wakiash caught her.

Wakiash said, "Wait. I will give you something." So he gave her a piece of mountain goat's fat. Wakiash said to Mouse, "I want the totem pole and the house. I want the dances and the songs."

Mouse said, "Wait until I come again."

Mouse went back into the house. She said, "I could find nobody." So the animal people tried again to dance. They tried three times. Each time, Chief sent Mouse out to see if some one was near. Each time, Mouse talked with Wakiash. The third time Mouse said, "When they begin to dance, jump into the room."

So the animal people began to dance. Then Wakiash sprang into the room. The dancers were ashamed. They had taken off their animal clothes

and looked like men. So the animal people were silent. Then Mouse said, "What does this man want?' Now Wakiash wanted the totem pole and the house. He wanted the dances and the songs. Mouse knew what Wakiash was thinking. Mouse told the animal people.

Chief said, "Let the man sit down. We will show him how to dance." So they danced. Then Chief asked Wakiash what kind of a dance he would like to choose. They were using masks for the dance. Wakiash wanted the Echo mask, and the Little Man mask, the little man who talks, talks, and quarrels with others. Mouse told the people what Wakiash was thinking.

Then Chief said, "You can take the totem pole and the house also. You can take the masks and dances, for one dance." Then Chief folded up the house very small. He put it in a dancer's headdress. Chief said, " When you reach home, throw down this bundle. The house will unfold and you can give a dance."

Then Wakiash went back to Raven. Wakiash climbed on Raven's back and went to sleep. When he awoke, Raven and Frog were gone. Wakiash was alone. It was night and the tribe was asleep.

Then Wakiash threw down the bundle. Behold! the house and totem pole were there. The whale painted on the house was blowing. The animals on the totem pole were making noises. At once the tribe woke up. They came to see Wakiash. Wakiash found he had been gone four years instead of four days.

Then Wakiash gave a great dance. He taught the people the songs. Echo came to the dance. He repeated all the sounds they made. When they finished the dance, behold! the house was gone. It went back to the animal people. Thus all the chiefs were ashamed because Wakiash had the best dance.

Then Wakiash made out of wood a house and another totem pole. They called it Kalakuyuwish, "the pole that holds up the sky."

How the Old Man Above Created the World (Shastika)

Long, long ago, when the world was so new that even the stars were dark, it was very, very flat. Chareya, Old Man Above, could not see through the dark to the new, flat earth. Neither could he step down to it because it was so far below him. With a large stone he bored a hole in the sky. Then through the hole he pushed down masses of ice and snow, until a great pyramid rose from the plain. Old Man Above climbed down through the hole he had made in the sky, stepping from cloud to cloud, until he could put his foot on top the mass of ice and snow. Then with one long step he reached the earth.

The sun shone through the hole in the sky and began to melt the ice and snow. It made holes in the ice and snow. When it was soft, Chareya bored with his finger into the earth, here and there, and planted the first trees. Streams from the melting snow watered the new trees and made them grow. Then he gathered the leaves which fell from the trees and blew upon them.

They became birds. He took a stick and broke it into pieces. Out of the small end he made fishes and placed them in the mountain streams. Of the middle of the sticky he made all the animals except the grizzly bear. From the big end of the stick came the grizzly bear, who was made master of all. Grizzly was large and strong and cunning. When the earth was new he walked upon two feet and carried a large club. So strong was Grizzly that Old Man Above feared the creature he had made. Therefore, so that he might be safe, Chareya hollowed out the pyramid of ice and snow as a tepee. There he lived for thousands of snows. The Indians knew he lived there because they could see the smoke curling from the smoke hole of his tepee. When the pale-face came. Old Man Above went away. There is no longer any smoke from the smoke hole. White men call the tepee Mount Shasta.

Old Mole's Creation (Shastika)

Long, long ago, before there was any earth. Old Mole burrowed underneath Somewhere, and threw up the earth which forms the world. Then Great Man created the people. But the Indians were cold.

Now in the east gleamed the white Fire Stone. Therefore Coyote journeyed eastward, and brought back the Fire Stone for the Indians. So people had fire.

In the beginning. Sun had nine brothers, all flaming hot like himself. But Coyote killed the nine brothers and so saved the world from burning up. But Moon also had nine brothers all made of ice, like himself, and the Night People almost froze to death. Therefore Coyote went away out on the eastern edge of the world with his flint-stone knife. He heated stones to keep his hands warm, and as the Moons arose, he killed one after another with his flint-stone knife, until he had slain nine of them. Thus the people were saved from freezing at night.

When it rains, some Indian, sick in heaven, is weeping. Long, long ago, there was a good young Indian on earth. When he died the Indians wept so that a flood came upon the earth, and drowned all people except one couple.

How Qawaneca Created the World (Chemetunne)

At first it was dark. There was neither wind nor rain. There were no people or animals. In the middle of the water, on a piece of land, sat Qawaneca. He sat by his fire breathing the smoke of burning cedar. On the edge of the land stood another god. Looking northward, he saw an ash tree. Looking southward, he saw a red cedar. Therefore the ash and red cedar are sacred above all other trees. Looking southwest, he saw something red. Said Qawaneca : "It must be land coming." At last the land came and touched the piece on which they sat. But it was unsteady. It trembled. Then Qawaneca pressed his hands over it, making it steady. He wanted to make more land but he did not wish sickness to be in it. He said: "Where many die, I will make much water and little land. Where few die, I will make much land and little water."

Qawaneca chose three rocks and two pieces of earth. He threw one rock into the water. Then he listened. It went down, down, down! He threw another rock ; then the third. Then he threw a piece of earth. He listened. He threw the other piece of earth. After the fifth throw, mighty waves arose. They dashed against the land, then receded. Thus were the tides formed.

Then more land came, but it was muddy. Man could not step on it. Soon footprints appeared. "Ha," said Qawaneca. " That is sickness. It is bad." So he made the water cover the land. Then he blew at the water and uncovered the land. Again footprints came in the mud. "That is bad. That is sickness," said Qawaneca. Four times he made water cover the land. The fifth time the footprints were made as before. Qawaneca let them alone. Five is a sacred number.

All this time it was dark. Qawaneca tried to make daylight, but could not. Then he called all the birds to a great council. He asked them how to make sunlight. Only one bird knew. He said in the far north was the sun. Two wild geese had been there. The geese said there was a magic way of calling the sun. They would teach Qawaneca if he would give special privileges to all birds. So Qawaneca learned the secret and called the sun. It came at his call and stopped as he told it. So Qawaneca made a track for the sun, northward in summer, southward in winter.

Qawaneca pulled two hairs from his head and threw them on the ground. They became snakes. Soon there were many on the land and in the water. They made storms by blowing with their mouths. One long serpent coiled itself five times around the world, so it does not fall apart.

Qawaneca pulled two more hairs from his head. They became dogs.

Afterwards a woman came from the south. She is the Mother who never dies. She is the South. All Indians return to her at death and she sends them back as infants. Qawaneca now lives in the sun and looks down on the people.

Genesis (Blackfoot)

All animals of the Plains at one time heard and knew him, and all birds of the air heard and knew him. All things that he had made understood him, when he spoke to them—the birds, the animals, and the people.

Old Man was travelling about, south of here, making the people. He came from the south, travelling north, making animals and birds as he passed along. He made the mountains, prairies, timber, and brush first. So he went along, travelling northward, making things as he went, putting rivers here and there, and falls on them, putting red paint here and there in the ground—fixing up the world as we see it today. He made the Milk River (the Teton) and crossed it, and, being tired, went up on a little hill and lay down to rest. As he lay on his back, stretched out on the ground, with arms extended, he marked himself out with stones—the shape of his body, head, legs, arms, and everything. There you can see those rocks today. After he had rested, he went on northward, and stumbled over a knoll and fell down on his knees. Then he said, "You are a bad thing to be stumbling against"; so he raised up two large buttes there, and named them the Knees, and they are called so to this day. He went on further north, and with some of the rocks he carried with him he built the Sweet Grass Hills.

Old Man covered the plains with grass for the animals to feed on. He marked off a piece of ground, and in it he made to grow all kinds of roots and berries—camas, wild carrots, wild turnips, sweet-root, bitter-root, sarvis berries, bull berries, cherries, plums, and rosebuds. He put trees in the ground. He put all kinds of animals on the ground. When he made the bighorn with its big head and horns, he made it out on the prairie. It did not seem to travel easily on the prairie; it was awkward and could not go fast. So he took it by one of its horns, and led it up into the mountains, and turned it loose; and it skipped about among the rocks, and went up fearful places with ease. So he said, "This is the place that suits you; this is what you are fitted for, the rocks and the mountains." While he was in the mountains, he made the antelope out of dirt, and turned it loose, to see how it would go. It ran so fast that it fell over some rocks and hurt itself.

Genesis (Blackfoot)

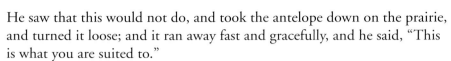

He saw that this would not do, and took the antelope down on the prairie, and turned it loose; and it ran away fast and gracefully, and he said, "This is what you are suited to."

One day Old Man determined that he would make a woman and a child; so he formed them both—the woman and the child, her son—of clay. After he had moulded the clay in human shape, he said to the clay, "You must be people," and then he covered it up and left it, and went away. The next morning he went to the place and took the covering off, and saw that the clay shapes had changed a little. The second morning there was still more change, and the third still more. The fourth morning he went to the place, took the covering off, looked at the images, and told them to rise and walk; and they did so. They walked down to the river with their Maker, and then he told them that his name was Napi, Old Man.

As they were standing by the river, the woman said to him, "How is it? will we always live, will there be no end to it?" He said: "I have never thought of that. We will have to decide it. I will take this buffalo chip and throw it in the river. If it floats, when people die, in four days they will become alive again; they will die for only four days. But if it sinks, there will be an end to them." He threw the chip into the river, and it floated. The woman turned and picked up a stone, and said: "No, I will throw this stone in the river; if it floats we will always live, if it sinks people must die, that they may always be sorry for each other." The woman threw the stone into the water, and it sank. "There," said Old Man, "you have chosen. There will be an end to them."

It was not many nights after, that the woman's child died, and she cried a great deal for it. She said to Old Man: "Let us change this. The law that you first made, let that be a law." He said: "Not so. What is made law must be law. We will undo nothing that we have done. The child is dead, but it cannot be changed. People will have to die."

That is how we came to be people. It is he who made us.

The first people were poor and naked, and did not know how to get a living. Old Man showed them the roots and berries, and told them that they could eat them; that in a certain month of the year they could peel the bark off some trees and eat it, that it was good. He told the people that the animals should be their food, and gave them to the people, saying, "These are your herds." He said: "All these little animals that live in the ground—rats, squirrels, skunks, beavers—are good to eat. You need not fear to eat of their flesh." He made all the birds that fly, and told the people that there was no harm in their flesh, that it could be eaten. The first people that he created he used to take about through the timber and swamps and over the prairies, and show them the different plants. Of a certain plant he would say, "The root of this plant, if gathered in a

certain month of the year, is good for a certain sickness." So they learned the power of all herbs. In those days there were buffalo. Now the people had no arms, but those black animals with long beards were armed; and once, as the people were moving about, the buffalo saw them, and ran after them, and hooked them, and killed and ate them. One day, as the Maker of the people was travelling over the country, he saw some of his children, that he had made, lying dead, torn to pieces and partly eaten by the buffalo. When he saw this he was very sad. He said: "This will not do. I will change this. The people shall eat the buffalo."

He went to some of the people who were left, and said to them, "How is it that you people do nothing to these animals that are killing you?" The people said: "What can we do? We have no way to kill these animals, while they are armed and can kill us." Then said the Maker: "That is not hard. I will make you a weapon that will kill these animals." So he went out, and cut some sarvis-berry shoots, and brought them in, and peeled the bark off them. He took a larger piece of wood, and flattened it, and tied a string to it, and made a bow. Now, as he was the master of all birds and could do with them as he wished, he went out and caught one, and took feathers from its wing, and split them, and tied them to the shaft of wood. He tied four feathers along the shaft, and tried the arrow at a mark, and found that it did not fly well. He took these feathers off, and put on three; and when he tried it again, he found that it was good. He went out and began to break sharp pieces off the stones. He tried them, and found that the black flint stones made the best arrow points, and some white flints. Then he taught the people how to use these things.

Then he said: "The next time you go out, take these things with you, and use them as I tell you, and do not run from these animals. When they run at you, as soon as they get pretty close, shoot the arrows at them, as I have taught you; and you will see that they will run from you or will run in a circle around you."

Now, as people became plenty, one day three men went out on to the plain to see the buffalo, but they had no arms. They saw the animals, but when the buffalo saw the men, they ran after them and killed two of them, but one got away. One day after this, the people went on a little hill to look about, and the buffalo saw them, and said, "*Saiyah*, there is some more of our food," and they rushed on them. This time the people did not run. They began to shoot at the buffalo with the bows and arrows Napi had given them, and the buffalo began to fall; but in the fight a person was killed.

At this time these people had flint knives given them, and they cut up the bodies of the dead buffalo. It is not healthful to eat the meat raw, so Old Man gathered soft dry rotten driftwood and made punk of it, and then got a piece of hard wood, and drilled a hole in it with an arrow point, and gave them a pointed piece of hard wood, and taught them how to make a fire with fire sticks, and to cook the flesh of these animals and eat it.

They got a kind of stone that was in the land, and then took another harder stone and worked one upon the other, and hollowed out the softer one, and made a kettle of it. This was the fashion of their dishes.

Also Old Man said to the people: "Now, if you are overcome, you may go and sleep, and get power. Something will come to you in your dream, that will help you. Whatever these animals tell you to do, you must obey them, as they appear to you in your sleep. Be guided by them. If anybody wants help, if you are alone and travelling, and cry aloud for help, your prayer will be answered. It may be by the eagles, perhaps by the buffalo, or by the bears. Whatever animal answers your prayer, you must listen to him." That was how the first people got through the world, by the power of their dreams.

After this, Old Man kept on, travelling north. Many of the animals that he had made followed him as he went. The animals understood him when he spoke to them, and he used them as his servants. When he got to the north point of the Porcupine Mountains, there he made some more mud images of people, and blew breath upon them, and they became people. He made men and women. They asked him, "What are we to eat?" He made many images of clay, in the form of buffalo. Then he blew breath on these, and they stood up; and when he made signs to them, they started to run. Then he said to the people, "Those are your food." They said to him, "Well, now, we have those animals; how are we to kill them?" "I will show you," he said. He took them to the cliff, and made them build rock piles like this; and he made the people hide behind these piles of rock, and said, "When I lead the buffalo this way, as I bring them opposite to you, rise up."

After he had told them how to act, he started on toward a herd of buffalo. He began to call them, and the buffalo started to run toward him, and they followed him until they were inside the lines. Then he dropped back; and as the people rose up, the buffalo ran in a straight line and jumped over the cliff. He told the people to go and take the flesh of those animals. They tried to tear the limbs apart, but they could not. They tried to bite pieces out, and could not. So Old Man went to the edge of the cliff, and broke some pieces of stone with sharp edges, and told them to cut the flesh with these. When they had taken the skins from these animals, they set up some poles and put the hides on them, and so made a shelter to sleep under. There were some of these buffalo that went over the cliff that were not dead. Their legs were broken, but they were still alive. The people cut strips of green hide, and tied stones in the middle, and made large mauls, and broke in the skulls of the buffalo, and killed them.

After he had taught those people these things, he started off again, travelling north, until he came to where Bow and Elbow rivers meet. There he made some more people, and taught them the same things. From here he again went on northward. When he had come nearly to the Red Deer's River, he reached the hill where the Old Man sleeps. There he lay down and rested himself. The form of his body is to be seen there yet.

When he awoke from his sleep, he travelled further northward and came to a fine high hill. He climbed to the top of it, and there sat down to rest. He looked over the country below him, and it pleased him. Before him the hill was steep, and he said to himself, "Well, this is a fine place for sliding; I will have some fun," and he began to slide down the hill. The marks where he slid down are to be seen yet, and the place is known to all people as the "Old Man's Sliding Ground."

This is as far as the Blackfeet followed Old Man. The Crees know what he did further north.

In later times once, Napi said, "Here I will mark you off a piece of ground," and he did so. Then he said: "There is your land, and it is full of all kinds of animals, and many things grow in this land. Let no other people come into it. This is for you five tribes (Blackfeet, Bloods, Piegans, Gros Ventres, Sarcees). When people come to cross the line, take your bows and arrows, your lances and your battle-axes, and give them battle and keep them out. If they gain a footing, trouble will come to you."

Our forefathers gave battle to all people who came to cross these lines, and kept them out. Of late years we have let our friends, the white people, come in, and you know the result. We, his children, have failed to obey his laws.

The Creation of the World (Pima)

In the beginning there was nothing at all except darkness. All was darkness and emptiness. For a long, long while, the darkness gathered until it became a great mass. Over this the spirit of Earth Doctor drifted to and fro like a fluffy bit of cotton in the breeze. Then Earth Doctor decided to make for himself an abiding place. So he thought within himself, "Come forth, some kind of plant," and there appeared the creosote bush. He placed this before him and set it upright. But it at once fell over. He set it upright again; again it fell. So it fell until the fourth time it remained upright. Then Earth Doctor took from his breast a little dust and flattened it into a cake. When the dust cake was still, he danced upon it, singing a magic song.

Next he created some black insects which made black gum on the creosote bush. Then he made a termite which worked with the small earth cake until it grew very large. As he sang and danced upon it, the flat world stretched out on all sides until it was as large as it is now. Then he made a round sky-cover to fit over it, round like the houses of the Pimas. But the earth shook and stretched, so that it was unsafe. So Earth Doctor made a gray spider which was to spin a web around the edges of the earth and sky, fastening them together. When this was done, the earth grew firm and solid.

Earth Doctor made water, mountains, trees, grass, and weeds—made everything as we see it now. But all was still inky blackness. Then he made a dish, poured water into it, and it became ice. He threw this round block of ice far to the north, and it fell at the place where the earth and sky were woven together. At once the ice began to gleam and shine. We call it now the sun. It rose from the ground in the north up into the sky and then fell back. Earth Doctor took it and threw it to the west where the earth and sky were sewn together. It rose into the sky and again slid back to the earth. Then he threw it to the far south, but it slid back again to the flat earth. Then at last he threw it to the east. It rose higher and higher in the sky until it reached the highest point in the round blue cover and began to slide down on the other side. And so the sun does even yet.

Then Earth Doctor poured more water into the dish and it became

ice. He sang a magic song, and threw the round ball of ice to the north where the earth and sky are woven together. It gleamed and shone, but not so brightly as the sun. It became the moon, and it rose in the sky, but fell back again, just as the sun had done. So he threw the ball to the west, and then to the south, but it slid back each time to the earth. Then he threw it to the east, and it rose to the highest point in the sky-cover and began to slide down on the other side. And so it does even today, following the sun.

But Earth Doctor saw that when the sun and moon were not in the sky, all was inky darkness. So he sang a magic song, and took some water into his mouth and blew it into the sky, in a spray, to make little stars. Then he took his magic crystal and broke it into pieces and threw them into the sky, to make the larger stars. Next he took his walking stick and placed ashes on the end of it. Then he drew it across the sky to form the Milky Way. So Earth Doctor made all the stars.

Beginning of Newness (Zuni)

Before the beginning of the New-making, the All-father Father alone had being. Through ages there was nothing else except black darkness.

In the beginning of the New-making, the All-father Father thought outward in space, and mists were created and up-lifted. Thus through his knowledge he made himself the Sun who was thus created and is the great Father. The dark spaces brightened with light. The cloud mists thickened and became water.

From his flesh, the Sun-father created the Seed-stuff of worlds, and he himself rested upon the waters. And these two, the Four-fold-containing Earth-mother and the All-covering Sky-father, the surpassing beings, with power of changing their forms even as smoke changes in the wind, were the father and mother of the soul-beings.

Then as man and woman spoke these two together. "Behold!" said Earth-mother, as a great terraced bowl appeared at hand, and within it water, "This shall be the home of my tiny children. On the rim of each world-country in which they wander, terraced mountains shall stand, making in one region many mountains by which one country shall be known from another."

Then she spat on the water and struck it and stirred it with her fingers. Foam gathered about the terraced rim, mounting higher and higher. Then with her warm breath she blew across the terraces. White flecks of foam broke away and floated over the water. But the cold breath of Sky-father shattered the foam and it fell downward in fine mist and spray.

Then Earth-mother spoke:

"Even so shall white clouds float up from the great waters at the borders of the world, and clustering about the mountain terraces of the horizon, shall be broken and hardened by thy cold. Then will they shed downward, in rain-spray, the water of life, even into the hollow places of my lap. For in my lap shall nestle our children, man-kind and creature-kind, for warmth in thy coldness."

So even now the trees on high mountains near the clouds and Sky-father, crouch low toward Earth-mother for warmth and protection. Warm is Earth-mother, cold our Sky-father.

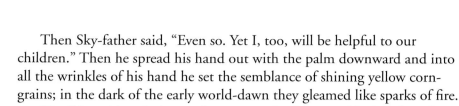

Beginning of Newness (Zuni)

Then Sky-father said, "Even so. Yet I, too, will be helpful to our children." Then he spread his hand out with the palm downward and into all the wrinkles of his hand he set the semblance of shining yellow corn-grains; in the dark of the early world-dawn they gleamed like sparks of fire.

"See," he said, pointing to the seven grains between his thumb and four fingers, "our children shall be guided by these when the Sun-father is not near and thy terraces are as darkness itself. Then shall our children be guided by lights." So Sky-father created the stars. Then he said, "And even as these grains gleam up from the water, so shall seed grain like them spring up from the earth when touched by water, to nourish our children." And thus they created the seed-corn. And in many other ways they devised for their children, the soul-beings.

But the first children, in a cave of the earth, were unfinished. The cave was of sooty blackness, black as a chimney at night time, and foul. Loud became their murmurings and lamentations, until many sought to escape, growing wiser and more man-like.

But the earth was not then as we now see it. Then the Sun-father sent down two sons (sons also of the Foam-cap), the Beloved Twain, Twin Brothers of Light, yet Elder and Younger, the Right and the Left, like to question and answer in deciding and doing. To them the Sun-father imparted his own wisdom. He gave them the great cloud-bow, and for arrows the thunderbolts of the four quarters. For buckler, they had the fog-making shield, spun and woven of the floating clouds and spray. The shield supports its bearer, as clouds are supported by the wind, yet hides its bearer also. And he gave to them the fathership and control of men and of all creatures. Then the Beloved Twain, with their great cloud-bow lifted the Sky-father into the vault of the skies, that the earth might become warm and fitter for men and creatures. Then along the sun-seeking trail, they sped to the mountains west ward. With magic knives they spread open the depths of the mountain and uncovered the cave in which dwelt the unfinished men and creatures. So they dwelt with men, learning to know them, and seeking to lead them out.

Now there were growing things in the depths, like grasses and vines. So the Beloved Twain breathed on the stems, growing tall toward the light as grass is wont to do, making them stronger, and twisting them upward until they formed a great ladder by which men and creatures ascended to a second cave.

Up the ladder into the second cave-world, men and the beings crowded, following closely the Two Little but Mighty Ones. Yet many fell back and were lost in the darkness. They peopled the under-world from which they escaped in after time, amid terrible earth shakings.

In this second cave it was as dark as the night of a stormy season, but larger of space and higher. Here again men and the beings increased, and

their complainings grew loud. So the Twain again increased the growth of the ladder, and again led men upward, not all at once, but in six bands, to become the fathers of the six kinds of men, the yellow, the tawny gray, the red, the white, the black, and the mingled. And this time also many were lost or left behind.

Now the third great cave was larger and lighter, like a valley in starlight. And again they increased in number. And again the Two led them out into a fourth cave. Here it was light like dawning, and men began to perceive and to learn variously, according to their natures, wherefore the Twain taught them first to seek the Sun-father.

Then as the last cave became filled and men learned to understand, the Two led them forth again into the great upper world, which is the World of Knowing and Seeing.

The Men of Early Times (Zuni)

Eight years was but four days and four nights when the world was new. It was while such days and nights continued that men were led out, in the night-shine of the World of Seeing. For even when they saw the great star, they thought it the Sun-father himself, it so burned their eyeballs.

Men and creatures were more alike then than now. Our fathers were black, like the caves they came from ; their skins were cold and scaly like those of mud creatures; their eyes were goggled like an owl's; their ears were like those of cave bats; their feet were webbed like those of walkers in wet and soft places; they had tails, long or short, as they were old or young. Men crouched when they walked, or crawled along the ground like lizards. They feared to walk straight, but crouched as before time they had in their cave worlds, that they might not stumble or fall in the uncertain light.

When the morning star arose, they blinked excessively when they beheld its brightness and cried out that now surely the Father was coming. But it was only the elder of the Bright Ones, heralding with his shield of flame the approach of the Sun-father. And when, low down in the east, the Sun-father himself appeared, though shrouded in the mist of the world-waters, they were blinded and heated by his light and glory. They fell down wallowing and covered their eyes with their hands and arms, yet ever as they looked toward the light, they struggled toward the Sun as moths and other night creatures seek the light of a camp fire. Thus they became used to the light. But when they rose and walked straight, no longer bending, and looked upon each other, they sought to clothe themselves with girdles and garments of bark and rushes. And when by walking only upon their hinder feet they were bruised by stone and sand, they plaited sandals of yucca fiber.

Spider's Creation (Sia)

In the beginning, long, long ago, there was but one being in the lower world. This was the spider, Sussistinnako. At that time there were no other insects, no birds, animals, or any other living creature.

The spider drew a line of meal from north to south and then crossed it with another line running east and west. On each side of the first line, north of the second, he placed two small parcels. They were precious but no one knows what was in them except Spider. Then he sat down near the parcels and began to sing. The music was low and sweet and the two parcels accompanied him, by shaking like rattles. Then two women appeared, one from each parcel.

In a short time people appeared and began walking around. Then animals, birds, and insects appeared, and the spider continued to sing until his creation was complete.

But there was no light, and as there were many people, they did not pass about much for fear of treading upon each other. The two women first created were the mothers of all. One was named Utset and she was the mother of all Indians. The other was Nowutset, and she was the mother of all other nations. While it was still dark, the spider divided the people into clans, saying to some, "You are of the Cora clan, and you are the first of all." To others he said, "You belong to the Coyote clan." So he divided them into their clans, the clans of the Bear, the Eagle, and other clans.

After Spider had nearly created the earth, Haarts, he thought it would be well to have rain to water it, so he created the Cloud People, the Lightning People, the Thunder People, and the Rainbow People, to work for the people of Haarts, the earth. He divided this creation into six parts, and each had its home in a spring in the heart of a great mountain upon whose summit was a giant tree. One was in the spruce tree on the Mountain of the North; another in the pine tree on the Mountain of the West; another in the oak tree on the Mountain of the South; and another in the aspen tree on the Mountain of the East; the fifth was on the cedar tree on the Mountain of the Zenith; and the last in an oak on the Mountain of the Nadir.

The spider divided the world into three parts: Haarts, the earth; Tinia,

the middle plain; and Hu-wa-ka, the upper plain. Then the spider gave to
these People of the Clouds and to the rainbow, Tinia, the middle plain.

Now it was still dark, but the people of Haarts made houses for
themselves by digging in the rocks and the earth. They could not build
houses as they do now, because they could not see. In a short time Utset
and Nowutset talked much to each other, saying, " We will make light,
that our people may see. We cannot tell the people now, but to-morrow
will be a good day and the day after to-morrow will be a good day,"
meaning that their thoughts were good. So they spoke with one tongue.
They said, "Now all is covered with darkness, but after a while we will
have light."

Then these two mothers, being inspired by Sussistinnako, the spider,
made the sun from white shell, turkis, red stone, and abalone shell. After
making the sun, they carried him to the east and camped there, since
there were no houses. The next morning they climbed to the top of a high
mountain and dropped the sun down behind it. After a time he began to
ascend. When the people saw the light they were happy.

When the sun was far off, his face was blue; as he came nearer, the face
grew brighter. Yet they did not see the sun himself, but only a large mask
which covered his whole body.

The people saw that the world was large and the country beautiful.
When the two mothers returned to the village, they said to the people,
"We are the mothers of all."

The sun lighted the world during the day, but there was no light at
night. So the two mothers created the moon from a slightly black stone,
many kinds of yellow stone, turkis, and a red stone, that the world might
be lighted at night. But the moon travelled slowly and did not always
give light. Then the two mothers created the Star People and made their
eyes of sparkling white crystal that they might twinkle and brighten the
world at night. When the Star People lived in the lower world they were
gathered into beautiful groups; they were not scattered about as they are
in the upper world.

How Silverfox Created the World (Atsugewi)

In the beginning there was nothing but water. Coyote and Silver-Fox lived above in the sky, where there was a world like this one. Silver-Fox was anxious to make things, but Coyote was opposed to this. Finally Silver-Fox got tired of Coyote and sent him one day to get wood. While he was gone, Silver-Fox took an arrow-flaker and made a hole in the upper world, and looked down on the sea below. When Coyote came back, Silver-Fox did not tell him about the hole he had made. Next day he sent Coyote off again for wood. While he was gone Silver-Fox thrust down the arrow-flaker and found that it reached to the water and down to the bottom of the water. So he climbed through the hole. As he came near the surface of the water, he made a little round island on which he stayed. When Coyote returned, he could not find Silver-Fox, and after hunting a long time, he began to feel remorseful. Finally he found the hole in the sky. He peeped through and saw Silver-Fox on his island, far, far below. He called to Silver-Fox he was sorry, and asked how to get down. Silver-Fox did not answer. Coyote said Silver-Fox ought not to treat him so badly; then Silver-Fox put up the arrow-flaker and Coyote came down.

But the island was very small, and there was not room enough for Coyote to stretch out. For some time they slept and when they awoke they were very hungry. For five days things continued this way; until at last Silver-Fox gave Coyote some sunflower seeds. He asked where they came from. Silver-Fox did not answer.

After five days more, Silver-Fox made the island a little larger so that Coyote could have room to stretch out. At last he went comfortably asleep. At once Silver-Fox got up, dressed himself finely, and then made a big sweat house. When it was all done, he woke Coyote, who was much surprised to see the sweat house. Silver-Fox told Coyote to sweep it out, to spread grass on the floor, and to go to sleep again. He did so, and Silver-Fox dressed up again. He put on a finely beaded shirt and leggings, and smoked and sang more. Then, going outside, he pushed with his foot, and stretched out the earth in all directions, first to the east, then to the north, then to the west, and last to the south. For five nights he repeated this, until the world became as large as it is today. Each day Silver-Fox told

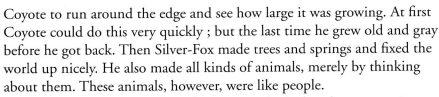

How Silverfox Created the World (Atsugewi)

Coyote to run around the edge and see how large it was growing. At first Coyote could do this very quickly ; but the last time he grew old and gray before he got back. Then Silver-Fox made trees and springs and fixed the world up nicely. He also made all kinds of animals, merely by thinking about them. These animals, however, were like people.

When the world was all made, Coyote asked what they were going to have for food. Silver-Fox did not reply. Coyote then said he thought there ought to be ten moons of winter in the year. Silver-Fox replied there would not be enough food for so long a winter. Coyote said it would be better not to have much food, that people could make soup out of dirt. Silver-Fox at first did not reply. Then Silver-Fox said it was not right to have ten moons of winter, that two were enough, and that people could then eat sunflower seeds, roots, and berries. Coyote repeated what he had said before, and they argued about it a long time. Finally Silver-Fox said: "You talk too much! I am going to make four moons for the whole year. I won't talk about it any more. There will be two moons of winter, and one of spring, and one of autumn. That's enough."

Creation of the World (Wyandot)

The people were living beyond the sky. They were Wyandots. One day the shaman told the people to dig around the roots of the wild apple tree standing by the chief's lodge and Indians at once began to dig. The chief's daughter was lying near by. As the men dug, a sudden noise startled them. They jumped back. They had broken through the floor of the Sky Land, and the tree and the chief's daughter fell through.

Now the world beneath was a great sheet of water. There was no land anywhere. Swans swimming about on the water heard a peal of thunder. It was the first peal ever heard in this world. When they looked upward, they saw the tree and the strange woman falling from the Sky Land. One of them said, " What strange thing is falling down?" Then he added, "The water will not hold her up. Let us swim together so she will fall upon our backs." So the chief's daughter fell upon their backs, and rested there.

After a while one swan said, "What shall we do with her? We cannot swim about this way very long." The other said, " Let us ask Big Turtle. He will probably call a council. Then we shall know what to do."

They swam around to Big Turtle and asked him what to do with the woman on their backs. Big Turtle at once sent a runner with a moccasin to the animals, so they came at once for a great council. The council talked a long while. Then someone stood up and asked about the tree. He said perhaps divers might go down and get just a little earth from its roots, if they knew where it had sunk. Big Turtle said, "Yes. If we can get earth, perhaps we might make an island for this woman." So the swans took them all to die place where the tree had fallen in the waste of waters.

Big Turtle called for divers. First down went Otter, the best of them all. He sank at once out of sight He was gone a long, long while. At last he came up, but he gasped and was dead. Then Muskrat was sent down. He also was gone a long, long while. Muskrat also died. Next Beaver was sent down to get earth from the roots of the tree. Beaver also was drowned. Many animals were drowned.

Big Turtle called, "Who will offer to go down for the earth?" No one offered himself, until at last Old Toad said she would try. All the animals laughed.

Old Toad was very small and very ugly. Big Turtle looked her over, but he said, "Well, you try then."

Down went Old Toad. At last they could not see her at all, though she went down slowly. Then they waited for her to come back. They waited, and waited, and waited. They began to say, "She will never come back." Then they saw a little bubble break on the water. Big Turtle said, "Let us swim there. That is where Old Toad is coming up." So it was done. Then Old Toad came slowly to the surface, close to Big Turtle. She opened her mouth and spat out a few grains of earth that fell on Big Turtle's shell. Old Toad was done for, too.

Small Turtle at once began to rub the earth around the edge of Big Turtle's shell. It began to grow into an island. The animals were looking on as it grew. Then the island became large enough for the woman to live on, so she stepped onto the earth. The island grew larger and larger, until it became as large as the world is today.

When an earthquake occurs, it is because Big Turtle moves his foot Sometimes he gets tired.

How the People got Five Fingers and Other Stories (Miwok)

All the world was dark.

Os-sa-le the Coyote-man and Pe-ta-le the Lizard-man were First People. They tried to make Indian people, each like himself. Os-sa-le said he was going to make man just like himself.

Pe-ta-le said that would be absurd ; "How could man eat or take hold of anything if he had no fingers?"

So they quarrelled, and Os-sa-le tried to kill Pe-ta-le ; but Pe-ta-le slid into a crack in a rock where Os-sa-le could not reach him. Then they talked and argued for a long time. After a while Pe-ta-le came out ahead and when they made people he gave them five fingers.

The world was dark and everybody wanted light and fire. By and by Pe-ta-le the Lizard said, "I see smoke down in the valley; who will go and get it? Loo'-loo-e the White-footed Mouse runs fast and plays the flute well; he had better go." So Loo'-loo-e went with his flute (*loo'-lah*) and found the home of the Valley People and played for them. They liked his music and gave a big feast and asked him to come into the roundhouse and play so that everyone might hear him.

We'-pi-ah'-gah the Eagle was chief of the Valley People and Wek'-wek the Falcon lived with him. When all the people had assembled and Loo'-loo-e the Mouse was there with his flute, Captain We'-pi-ah'-gah took the big feather blanket called *kook'-si-u*, made of feathers of Mol'-luk the Condor, and closed the doorway with it and made it very tight, for he had a feeling that Loo'- loo-e might try to steal something and run off with it.

Then Loo'-loo-e took his flute and began to play; he lay on his back and rocked to and fro and played for a long time. Everyone liked the music and felt happy. In a little while they all became sleepy. Soon Loo'-loo-e looked around and saw that they were asleep ; but he kept on playing till everybody was sound asleep. Then he got up and went to the fire and stole it all—two small coals—and put them in his flute and started to run away. But he could not get out of the roundhouse because of the thick feather blanket which We-pi-ah'-gah had hung over the doorway. So he stopped and cut a hole through it with his teeth and then ran out and hurried toward the mountains.

X2901-08

After a while the people awoke and found that the fire was gone. They were sure that Loo'-loo-e the Mouse had stolen it, and said, "Whom can we send who is fast enough to overtake him? Of all our people only Sah'-win-ne the Hail and Nuk'-kah the Shower are fast enough." So they sent these two to catch him. They rushed off toward the mountains and overtook him.

He saw them coming and put one coal in the oo'-noo tree (buckeye) and threw the other in the water. When Sah'-win-ne and Nuk'-kah caught him they could not find the coals. He told them to look, he had nothing. They looked and found nothing, and went back and told the Valley People. Then Loo'-loo-e took the coal from the oo'noo tree and put it back in his flute and ran up into the mountains with it and gave it to his people, and they put it in the middle of the roundhouse. Before this their country was dark, and they had always eaten their food raw. Now they could see and could cook meat.

Then Os-sa-le the Coyote-man brought the intestines of a deer and put them on the fire, covering it up and nearly putting it out. Because of his selfishness in doing this the people changed his name from Os-sa-le to Kat'-wah (greedy), which they call him to this day.

Then the people felt cold and only those in the middle of the roundhouse could talk as they had talked before. Those around the sides were so cold that their teeth chattered and they could not talk plainly. They separated into four groups on the four sides of the house—one on the north, one on the south, one on the east, and one on the west—and each group began to speak differently from the others, and also differently from the one in the middle. This is the way the speech of the people began to break up into five languages, and this is the way the five tribes began—the people being driven apart by the selfishness of Coyote.

The Evil Maker (Ojibwa)

The Great Spirit made man, and all the good things in the world, while the Evil Spirit was asleep. When the Evil Spirit awoke he saw an Indian, and, wondering at his appearance, he went to him and asked—

"Who made you?"

"The Great Spirit," replied the man.

"Oh, oh," thought the Evil Spirit, "if he can make such a being so can I."

So he went to work, and tried his best to make an Indian like the man he saw, but he made some mistake, and only made a black man. When he saw that he had failed he was very angry, and in that state was walking about when he met a black bear.

"Who made you?" he asked.

"The Great Spirit," answered the bear.

"Then," thought the Evil Spirit, "I will make a bear too."

To work he went, but do what he would he could not make a black bear, but only a grizzly one, unfit for food. More disgusted than before, he was walking through the forest when he found a beautiful serpent.

"Who made you?" he asked.

"The Great Spirit," replied the serpent.

"Then I will make some like you," said the Evil Maker.

He tried his best, but the serpents he made were all noisome and poisonous, and he saw that he had failed again.

Then it occurred to him that he might make some trees and flowers, but all his efforts only resulted in his producing some poor deformed trees and weeds.

Then he said—

"It is true, I have failed in making things like the Great Spirit, but I can at least spoil what he has made."

And he went off to put murder and lies in the hearts of men.

Legend of the Corn (Arikara)

The Arikara were the first to find the maize. A young man went out hunting. He came to a high hill. Looking down a valley, he saw a buffalo bull near where two rivers joined. When the young man looked to see how he could kill the buffalo, he saw how beautiful the country was. The banks of the two rivers were low, with many trees. The buffalo faced the north ; therefore he could not get within bow shot of him. He thought he should wait until the buf falo mored close to the banks of one of the rivers, or to a ravine where there were bushes and shrubs. So the young man waited. The sun went down before the buf falo moved.

Nearly all night the hunter lay awake. He had little food. He felt sorry he could not reach the buffalo. Before the sun rose, he hurried to the top of the hill. The buffalo stood just where it had, but it faced the east. Again he waited for it to move. He waited all day. When the sun went down, the buffalo still stood in the same place.

Nearly all night the young man lay awake. He had very little food indeed. The next morning he rose early, and came to the top of the hill, just as the sun came up. The buffalo was still standing in the same place; but now it faced the south. He waited all day. Then the sun went down.

Now the next morning, when he arose early, the buffalo stood in the same place; this time it faced the west. All day the young man waited, but the buffalo did not move.

Now the young man thought, " Why does not the buffalo move? " He saw it did not drink, did not eat, did not sleep. He thought some power must be influencing it.

Now the next morning, the young man hurried to the top of the hill. The sun had risen and everything was light. The buffalo was gone. Then he saw where the buffalo had stood there was a strange bush.

He went to the place ; then he saw it was a plant. He looked for the tracks of the buffalo. He saw where it had turned to the east and to the south and to the west. In the center there was one track; out of it the small plant had grown. There was no track to show where the buffalo had left the place.

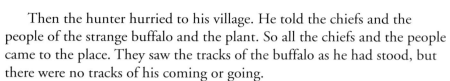

Legend of the Corn (Arikara)

Then the hunter hurried to his village. He told the chiefs and the people of the strange buffalo and the plant. So all the chiefs and the people came to the place. They saw the tracks of the buffalo as he had stood, but there were no tracks of his coming or going.

So all the people knew that Wahkoda had given this strange plant to the people. They knew of other plants they might eat. They knew there was a time when each plant was ripe. So they watched the strange plant; they guarded it and protected it.

Then a flower appeared on the plant. Afterwards, at one of the joints, a new part of the plant pushed out. It had hair. At first the hair was green; then it was brown. Then the people thought, "Perhaps this fruit is ripe." But they did not dare touch it. They met together. They looked at the plant.

Then a young man said, "My life has not been good. If any evil comes to me, it will not matter."

So the people were willing, and the young man put his hand on the plant and then on its fruit. He grasped the fruit boldly. He said to the people, "It is solid. It is ripe." Then he pulled apart the husks, and said, "It is red."

He took a few of the grains and showed them to the people. He ate some. He did not die. So the people knew Wahkoda had sent this plant to them for food.

Now in the fall, when the prairie grass turned brown, the leaves of this plant turned brown also. Then the fruit was plucked, and put away. After the winter was over, the kernels were divided. There were four to each family.

Then the people moved the lodges to the place where the plant had grown. When the hills became green, they planted the seed of the strange plant. But first they built little mounds like the one out of which it grew. So the fruit grew and ripened. It had many colors; red, and yellow, and white, and blue.

Then the next year there were many plants and many ears of corn. So they sent to other tribes. They invited them to visit them and gave them of the new food. Thus the Omahas came to have corn.

Yo-Sem-i-Te, Large Grizzly Bear (Yosemite)

When the world was made, the Great Spirit tore out the heart of Kay-o-pha, the Sky Mountains, and left the gash unhealed. He sent the Coyote to people the valley with a strong and hardy race of men, who called their home Ah-wah-nee, and themselves, the Ah- wah-nee-chees.

The Ah-wah-nee-chees lived the simple, savage life, which knows no law but to hunt and kill and eat. By day the trackless forests rang with the clamor of the chase. By the flaring light of their fires the hunters gorged themselves upon the fresh-killed meat, feasting far into the night. They made war upon the tribes that lived beyond the walls of Ah-wah-nee and never knew defeat, for none dared follow them to their rock-ribbed fastness. They were feared by all save the outcasts of other tribes, whose lawless deeds won for them a place among the Ah-wah-nee-chees. Thus the children of Ah-wah-nee increased in number and strength.

As time went by, the Ah-wah-nee-chees, in their pride of power, forgot the Great Spirit who had given them their stronghold and made them feared of all their race. And the Great Spirit, turning upon them in his wrath, loosed his evil forces in their midst, scourging them with a black sickness that swept all before it as a hot wind blights the grain at harvest time.

The air of the valley was a poison breath, in which the death shade hovered darkly. Before the Evil Spirit medicine men were powerless. Their mystic spells and incantations were a weird mockery, performed among the dying and the dead; and when at last the Evil One passed onward in his cursed flight, the once proud and powerful band of Ah-wah-nee-chees was like a straggling pack of gaunt gray wolves. Their eyes gleamed dully in their shrunken faces, and the skin hung in loose folds on their wasted bodies.

Those who were able fled from the valley, which was now a haunted place, eerie with flitting shadows of funeral fires and ghostly echoes of the funeral wail. They scattered among the tribes beyond the mountains, and Ah-wah-nee was deserted.

A vast stillness settled upon the valley, broken only by the songs of birds and the roar of Cho-look when Spring sent the mountain torrents

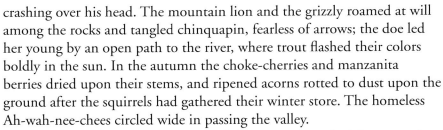

Yo-Sem-i-Te, Large Grizzly Bear (Yosemite)

crashing over his head. The mountain lion and the grizzly roamed at will among the rocks and tangled chinquapin, fearless of arrows; the doe led her young by an open path to the river, where trout flashed their colors boldly in the sun. In the autumn the choke-cherries and manzanita berries dried upon their stems, and ripened acorns rotted to dust upon the ground after the squirrels had gathered their winter store. The homeless Ah-wah-nee-chees circled wide in passing the valley.

Over beyond To-co-yah, the North Dome, among the Mo-nos and Pai-u-tes, a few of the ill-fated Ah-wah-nee-chees had found refuge. Among them was the chief of the tribe, who after a time took a Mo-no maiden for his bride. By this Mo-no woman he had a son, and they gave him the name of Ten-ie-ya. Before another round of seasons, the spirit of the Ah-wah-nee-chee chieftain had wandered on to the Land of the Sun, the home of happy souls.

Ten-ie-ya grew up among his mother's people, but the fire of a warrior chief was in his blood and he liked not to live where the word of another was law. The fire in his blood was kept aflame by the words of an old man, the patriarch of his father's tribe, who urged him to return to Ah-wah-nee, the home of his ancestors, and gather about him the people whose chief he was by right of birth.

So Ten-ie-ya went back across the mountains by a trail abandoned long ago, and from the camps of other tribes came those in whose veins was any trace of Ah-wah-nee-chee blood; and, as before, the number was increased by lawless braves of weaker bands who liked a greater freedom for their lawlessness. Again, under the favor of the Great Spirit, the Ah-wah-nee-chees flourished and by their fierce strength and daring became to other tribes as the mountain lion to the wolf and the coyote and the mountain sheep.

And it chanced that one day while Ten-ie-ya and his warriors were camped near Le-ham-i-te, the Canon of the Arrow-wood, a young brave went out in the early morning to the lake of Ke-koo-too-yem, the Sleeping Water, to spear fish. His lithe, strong limbs took no heed of the rocky talus in his path, and he leaped from boulder to boulder, following the wall that rose sheer above him and cut the blue sky overhead.

As he reached the base of Scho-ko-ni, the cliff that arches like the shade of an Indian cradle basket, he came suddenly upon a monster grizzly that had just crept forth from his winter cave. The grizzly knows no man for his friend; least of all, the man who surprises him at the first meal after his long sleep. The rivals of Ah-wah-nee were face to face.

The Ah-wah-nee-chee had no weapon save his fish spear, useless as a reed; yet he had the fearlessness of youth and the courage of a race to whom valorous deeds are more than strings of wampum, piles of pelt or many cattle. He faced the grizzly boldly as the clumsy hulk rose to its full

height, at bay and keen for attack. With instinctive love of conflict roused, the young chief seized a broken limb that lay at his feet, and gave the grizzly blow for blow.

The claws of the maddened brute raked his flesh. The blood ran warm over his glistening skin and matted the bristled yellow fur of the grizzly.

The Ah-wah-nee-chee fought bravely. While there was blood in his body, he could fight; when the blood was gone, he could die; but with the traditions of his ancestors firing his brain, he could not flee from the young chief's club and by the blood from the young chief's torn flesh, the grizzly struggled savagely. He, too, was driven by the law of his breed, the universal law of the forest, the law of Indian and grizzly alike, which is to kill.

Such a battle could not last. With a low growl the crippled grizzly brought himself together and struck with the full force of his powerful arm. The blow fell short.

Yo-Sem-i-Te, Large Grizzly Bear (Yosemite)

Urging his waning strength to one last effort, the Ah-wah-nee-chee raised his club high above his head and brought it down with a heavy, well-aimed stroke that crushed the grizzly's skull and sent him rolling among the boulders, dead.

That night as the Ah-wah-nee-chees feasted themselves on bear meat, the story of the young chief's bravery was told, and told again; and from that hour he was known as Yo-sem-i-te, the Large Grizzly Bear.

In time the name Yo-sem-i-te was given to all the tribe of Ah-wah-nee-chees, who for fearlessness and lawlessness were rivaled only by the grizzly with whom they shared their mountain fastness. And when long afterward the white man came and took Ah-wah-nee for his own, he gave it the name by which Ten-ie-ya's band was known; and Cho-look, the high fall that makes the earth tremble with its mighty roar, he also called by the name of the Large Grizzly Bear, Yo-sem-i-te.

Heroes and Tricksters

The Raven Myth (Inuit)

It was in the time when there were no people on the earth plain. The first man for four days lay coiled up in the pod of the beach pea. On the fifth day he stretched out his feet and burst the pod. He fell to the ground and when he stood up he was a full-grown man. Man looked all around him and then at himself. He moved his hands and arms, his neck and legs. When he looked back he saw, still hanging to the vine, the pod of the beach pea, with a hole in the lower end out of which he had dropped. When he looked about him again, he saw that he was getting farther from his starting place. The ground seemed to move up and down under his feet, and it was very soft. After a while he had a strange feeling in his stomach, so he stooped down to drink some water from a small pool at his feet. Then he felt better.

When Man looked up again he saw coming toward him, with a fluttering motion, something dark. He watched the dark thing until it stopped just in front of him. It was Raven.

As soon as Raven stopped, he raised one of his wings and pushed up his beak, as though it were a mask, to the top of his head. Thus Raven changed at once into a man. Raven stared hard at Man, moving from side to side to see him better.

Raven said, "What are you? Where did you come from? I have never seen anything like you."

Raven still stared at Man, surprised to find this new thing so much like himself. He made Man walk around a little, while he perked his head from side to side to see him better. Then Raven said again, in astonishment, "Where did you come from? I have never seen anything like you before."

Man said, "I came from the pea pod." He pointed to the plant from which he came.

"Ah, I made that vine," said Raven. " But I did not know that anything like you would come from it. Come with me to the high ground over there; it is thicker and harder. 'This ground I made later and it is soft and thin."

So Man and Raven walked to the higher ground which was firm and hard. Raven asked Man if he had eaten anything. Man said he had taken

some of the soft stuff from one of the pools.

"Ah, you drank some water," said Raven. "Now wait for me here."

Raven drew down his beak, as though it were a mask, over his face. He at once became a bird and flew far up into the sky, far out of sight. Man waited until the fourth day. Then Raven returned bringing four berries in his claws. He pushed up his beak and so became a man again. Then he gave to Man two salmon berries and two heath berries, saying, "Here is something I made for you to eat. I wish them to be plentiful on the earth. Eat them."

Man put the berries into his mouth, one after the other, and ate them. Then he felt better. Then Raven left Man near a small creek while he went to the edge of the water. He took two pieces of clay at the water's edge, and shaped them like a pair of mountain sheep. He held them in his hand until they were dry, and then he called Man to come and see them. Man said they were pretty, so Raven told him to close his eyes. Man closed his eyes tightly. Then Raven pulled down his beak-mask, and waved his wings four times over the pieces of clay. At once they bounded away as full-grown mountain sheep. Raven told Man to look.

Man was so much pleased that Raven said, "If these animals are plentiful perhaps people will try to kill them."

Man said, "Yes."

Then Raven said, "Well, it will be better for them to live among the steep rocks so every one cannot kill them. There only shall they be found."

Raven took two more pieces of clay and shaped them like tame reindeer. He held them in his hand until they were partly dry, then told Man to look at them. Raven again drew down his beak-mask and waved his wings four times over them. Thus they became alive, but as they were only dry in spots while Raven held them, therefore they remained brown and white, with mottled coat. Raven told Man these tame reindeer would be very few in number.

Again Raven took two pieces of clay and shaped them like the caribou or wild reindeer. But he held them in his hands only a little while so that only the bellies of the reindeer became dry and white. Then Raven drew down his beak-mask, and waved his wings over them, and they bounded away. But because only their bellies were dry and white while Raven held them, therefore the wild reindeer is brown except its white belly.

Raven said to Man, "These animals will be very common. People will kill many of them."

Thus Raven began to create the animals.

Raven said one day to Man, "You are lonely by yourself. I will make you a companion." He went to some white clay at a spot distant from the clay of which he had made animals, and made of the clay a figure almost like Man. Raven kept looking at Man while he shaped the figure. Then he took fine water grass from the creek and fastened it on the back of the head for hair. When the clay was shaped, Raven drew down his beak-mask and waved his wings over it. The clay became a beautiful girl. The girl was white and fair because Raven let the clay dry entirely before he waved his wings over it.

Raven took the girl to Man. " There is a companion for you," he said.

Now in the days of the first people on the earth plain, there were no mountains far or near. No rain ever fell and there were no winds. The sun shone always very brightly.

Then Raven showed the first people on the earth plain how to sleep warmly in the dry moss when they were tired. Raven himself drew down his beak-mask and went to sleep like a bird.

When Raven awakened, he went back to the creek. Here he made two sticklebacks, two graylings, and two blackfish. When these were swimming about in the water, he called Man to see them. Man raised his hand in surprise and the sticklebacks darted away. Raven told him the graylings would be found in clear mountain streams, while the sticklebacks would live along the coast, and that both would be good for food.

Raven next made the shrewmouse. He said, "The shrewmouse will not be good for food. It will prevent the earth plain from looking bare and cheerless."

In this way Raven was busy several days, making birds and fishes and animals. He showed each of them to Man and explained what they were good for. Then Raven flew into the sky, far, far away, and was gone four days. When he came back he brought a salmon to Man.

But Raven noticed that the ponds and lakes were silent and lonely, so he made water bugs to flit upon the surface of the water. He also made the beaver and the muskrat to live around the borders of the ponds. Raven told Man that the beavers would live along the streams and build strong houses, so Man must build a strong house also. Raven said the beavers would be very cunning and only good hunters could catch them. He also told Man how to catch the muskrat and how to use its skin for clothing.

Raven also made flies and mosquitoes and other insects to make the earth plain more cheerful. At first mosquitoes were like flies; they did not bite. One day Man killed a deer. After he had cut it up and placed the fat on a bush, he fell asleep. When he awoke he found the mosquitoes had eaten all of it Then Man was very angry and scolded the mosquitoes. He said, "Never eat meat again. Eat men." Before that mosquitoes never bit people.

When the first baby came on the earth plain. Raven rubbed it all over with white clay. He told Man it would grow into a man like himself. The next morning the baby was a big boy. He ran around pulling up grass and

The Raven Myth (Inuit)

flowers that Raven had planted. By the third day the baby was a full-grown man.

Then another baby was born on the earth plain. She was rubbed over with the white clay., The next day the baby was a big girl, walking around. On the third day she was a full-grown woman.

Now Raven began to be afraid that men would kill all the creatures he had made. He was afraid they would kill them for food and clothing. Therefore Raven went to a creek nearby. He took white clay and shaped it like a bear. Then he waved his wings over it, and the clay became a bear. But Raven jumped very quickly to one side when the bear became alive because it looked fiercely around and growled. Then Raven showed the bear to Man and told him to be careful.

He said the bear was very fierce and would tear him to pieces if he disturbed it.

Then Raven made the seals, and taught Man how to catch them. He also taught Man how to make strong lines from sealskin, and snares for the deer.

Then Raven went away to the place of the pea vine.

When he reached the pea vine he found three other men had just fallen from the same pod that Man had fallen from. These men were looking about them in wonder. Raven led them away from the pea vine, but in a different direction from the first man. He brought them close to the sea. Raven stayed with these three men a long time. He taught them how to take wood from the bushes and small trees he planted in hollows and sheltered places, and to make a fire drill, and also a bow. He made many more plants and birds which like the seacoast, but he did not make so many as in the land where Man lived. He taught these men how to make bows and arrows, spears and nets, and how to use them; and also how to capture the seals, which were now plentiful in the sea. Then he taught them how to make kayaks, and how to build houses of drift logs and of bushes, covered with earth. Then he made wives for these men, and went back to Man.

When Raven reached the land where Man lived, he thought the earth plain still looked bare. So, while the Others slept, Raven planted birch and spruce and cottonwood trees to grow in the low places. Then he woke up the people, who were pleased with the trees.

Then Raven taught Man how to make fire with the fire drill, and to place the spark of tinder in a bunch of dry grass and to wave it about until it blazed, and then to put dry wood upon it. He showed them how to roast fish on a stick, and how to make fish traps of splints and willow bark, and how to dry salmon for winter use.

Where Man lived there was now a large village because the people did everything as Raven told them, and therefore all the babies grew up in three days. One day Raven came back and sat down by Man by the creek and they talked of many things. Man asked Raven about the skyland. Man wanted to see the skyland which Raven had made. Therefore Raven took Man to the land in the sky.

Man found that the skyland was a very beautiful country, and that it had a much better climate than his land. But the people who lived there were very small. Their heads did not reach to Man's hips. The people wore fur clothing, with beautiful patterns, such as people on earth now wear, because Man showed his people how to make them. In the lakes were strange animals which would have killed Man if he had tried to drink of the water. In a dry lake bed, thickly covered with tall grass, Man saw a wonderful animal resting upon the tips of the grasses. It had a long head and six legs. It had fine, thick hair, and on the back of the head were two thick, short horns which bent forward and then curved back at the tips. Raven told Man it took many people to kill this animal.

Then they came to a round hole in the sky and around the edge of the hole was short grass, glowing like fire. Raven said, "This is the star called the moon-dog." Some of the grass had been pulled up. Raven said he had taken some to start the first fire on earth.

Then Raven said to Man, "Shut your eyes. I will take you to another country." Man climbed upon Raven's back and they dropped down through the star hole. They floated a long, long time through the air, then they floated through something else. When they stopped Raven saw he was at the bottom of the sea. Man could breathe there, but it seemed foggy. Raven said that was the appearance of the water. Then Raven said, "I want to make some new animals here ; but you must not walk about. You lie down and if you get tired, turn over on the other side."

Man went to sleep lying on one side, and slept a long while. When he waked up, he wanted to turn over, but he could not. Then Man thought, "I wish I could turn over," and at once he turned. As he turned, he was surprised to see that his body was covered with long, white hairs ; and his fingers were long claws. Then he went to sleep again. This he did three times more. Then when he woke up, Raven stood by him. Raven said, "I have changed you into a white bear. How do you like it? " Man could not make a sound until Raven waved his wings over him. Then he said he did not like it; if he was a bear he would have to live on the sea, while his son lived on land; so Man should feel badly. Then Raven struck the white skin with his wings and it fell off. So Man became himself again. But Raven took the empty bearskin, and placed one of his own tail feathers inside it for a spine. Then he waved his wing over it, and a white bear arose. Ever since then white bears have been found on the frozen sea.

Raven said, "How many times did you turn over?"

Man said, "Four."

Raven said, "You slept just four years."

Then Raven made other animals. He made the a-mi-kuk, a large, slimy animal, with thick skin, and with four long, wide-spreading arms. This is a fierce animal and lives in the sea. It wraps its four long arms around a man or a kayak and drags it under the water. A man cannot escape it. If he climbs out of his kayak on the ice, the a-mi-kuk will dart underneath and break the ice. If Man runs away on shore, the a-mi-kuk pursues him by burrowing through the earth.

No man can escape from it when once it pursues him.

Then Raven showed Man the walrus, and the dog walrus, with head and teeth like a dog. It always swam with large herds of walrus and with a stroke of its tail could kill a man. He showed him whales and the grampus. Raven told Man that only good hunters could kill a whale, but when one was killed an entire village could feast on it. He showed him also the sea fox, which is so fierce it kills men; and the sea otter, which is like the land otter but has finer fur, tipped with white, and other fishes and animals as they rose to the surface of the water.

Then Raven said, "Close your eyes. Hold fast to me.

Then Man found himself on the shore near his home. The village was very large. His wife was very old and his son was an old man. The people gave him place of honor in the kashim, and made him their headsman. So Man taught the young men many things.

Now Man wanted again to see the skyland, so Raven and Man went up among the dwarf people and lived there a long time. But on earth the village grew very large; the men killed many animals.

Now in those days, the sun shone always very brightly. No rain ever fell and no winds blew.

Man and Raven were angry because the people killed many animals. They took a long line and a grass basket, one night, and caught ten reindeer which they put into the basket. Now in those days reindeer had sharp teeth, like dogs. The next night Raven took the reindeer and let them down on the earth close to Man's village. Raven said, " Break down the first house you see and kill the people. Men are becoming too many." The reindeer did as Raven commanded. They stamped on the house and broke it down. They ate up the people with their sharp, wolf-like teeth. The next night. Raven let the reindeer down; again they broke down a house and ate up the people with their sharp teeth.

The village people were much frightened. The third night they covered the third house with a mixture of deer fat and berries. On the third night when the reindeer began to tear down the third house, their mouths were filled with the fat and sour berries. Then the reindeer ran away, shaking their heads so violently that all their long, sharp teeth fell out. Ever since

then reindeer have had small teeth and cannot harm people.

After the reindeer ran away. Raven and Man returned to the skyland. Man said, "If the people do not stop killing so many animals, they will kill everything you have made. It would be better to take the sun away from them. Then it will be dark and people will die."

Raven said, "That is right. You stay here. I will go and take away the sun."

So Raven went away and took the sun out of the sky. He put it in a skin bag and carried it far away, to a distant part of the skyland. Then it became dark on earth.

The people on earth were frightened when the sun vanished. They offered Raven presents of food and furs if he would bring back the sun. Raven said, "No." After a while Raven felt sorry for them, so he let them have a little light. He held up the sun in one hand for two days so people could hunt and secure food. Then he put the sun in the skin bag again and the earth was dark. Then, after a long time, when the people made him many gifts, he would let them have a little light again.

Now Raven had a brother living in the village. He was sorry for the earth people. So Raven's brother thought a long time. Then he died. The people put him in a grave box and had a burial feast. Then they left the grave box. At once Raven's brother slipped out of the box and went away from the village. He hid his raven mask and coat in a tree. Soon Raven's wife came for water. When she took up a dipperful to drink, Raven's brother, by magic, became a small leaf. He fell into the water and Raven's wife swallowed him

When Raven-Boy was born he grew very rapidly. He was running about when he was only a few days old. He cried for the sun which was in the skin bag, hanging on the rafters. Raven was fond of the boy so he let him play with the sun ; yet he was afraid Raven-Boy would lose the sun, so he watched him. When Raven-Boy began to play out of doors, he cried and begged for the sun. Raven said, "No." Then Raven-Boy cried more than ever. At last Raven gave him the sun in the house. Raven-Boy played with it a long while. When no one was looking, he ran quickly out of the house. He ran to the tree, put on his raven mask and coat, and flew far away with the sun in the skin bag. When Raven-Boy was far up in the sky, he heard Raven call, "Do not hide the sun. Let it out of the bag. Do not keep it always dark." Raven thought the boy had stolen it for himself.

Raven-Boy flew to the place where the sun belonged. He tore off the skin covering and put the sun in its place. Then he saw a broad path leading far away. He followed it to the side of a hole fringed with short, bright grass. He remembered that Raven had said, "Do not keep it always dark," therefore he made the sky turn, with all the stars and the sun. Thus it is now sometimes dark and sometimes light.

Raven-Boy picked some of the short, bright grass by the edge of the sky hole and stuck it into the sky. This is the morning star.

Raven-Boy went down to the earth. The people were glad to see him. They said, "What has become of Man who went into the skyland with Raven? " Now this was the first time that Raven-Boy had heard of Man. He started to fly up into the sky, but he could get only a small distance above the earth. When he found he could not get back to the sky, Raven-Boy wandered to the second village, where lived the men who had come from the pod of the beach pea. Raven-Boy there married a wife and he had many children. But the children could not fly to the sky. They had lost the magic power. Therefore the ravens now flutter over the tundras like other birds.

The Flood (Tlingit)

Long, long ago, in the days of the animal people, Raven-at-the-head-of-Nass became angry. He said, "Let rain pour down all over the world. Let people die of starvation." At once it became so stormy people could not get food, so they began to starve. Their canoes were also broken up, their houses fell in upon them, and they suffered very much. Then Nas-ca-ki-yel, Raven-at-the-head-of-Nass, asked for his jointed dance hat. When he put it on water began pouring out of the top of it. It is from Raven that the Indians obtained this kind of a hat.

When the water rose to the house floor, Raven and his mother climbed upon the lowest retaining timber. This house we are speaking of, although it looked like a house to them, was really part of the world. It had eight rows of retaining timbers.

When Raven and his mother climbed to a higher timber, the people of the world were climbing into the hills. Then Raven and his mother climbed to the fourth timber; by that time the water was half-way up the mountains. When the house was nearly full of water, Raven's mother got into the skin of a cax. To this very day Tlingits do not eat the cax because it was Raven's mother. Then Raven got into the skin of a white bird with copper-colored bill. Now the cax is a diver and stayed upon the surface of the water. But Raven flew to the very highest cloud and hung there by his bill. But his tail was in the water.

After Raven had hung in the cloud for days and days—nobody knows how long—he pulled his bill out and prayed to fall on a piece of kelp. He thought the water had gone down. When Raven fell upon the kelp and flew away he found the waters just half-way down the mountains.

Raven flew around until he met a shark, which had been swimming around with a long stick. Raven took the stick and climbed down it as a ladder to the bottom of the ocean. But Raven had set Eagle to watch the tide.

Raven wandered around the bottom of the ocean until he came to an old woman. He said to her, "How cold I am after eating those sea urchins." He repeated this over and over again.

At last the woman said, "What low tide is this Raven talking about?"

The Flood (Tlingit)

Raven did not answer. The woman kept repeating, "What low tide are you talking about?"

Then Raven became angry. He said, "I will stick these sea urchins into you if you don't keep quiet." At last he did so.

Then the woman began singing, "Don't, Raven! The tide will go down if you don't stop."

But the water was receding, as Raven had told it to, in his magic words. Raven asked Eagle, who was watching the tide, "How far down is the tide now?"

"The tide is as far down as half a man."

"How far down is the tide?" he asked again.

"The tide is very low," said Eagle.

Then the old woman started her magic song again.

Raven said, "Let it get dry all around the world."

After a while, Eagle said, "The tide is very low now. You can hardly see any water."

Raven said, "Let it get still drier."

At last everything was dry. This is the lowest tide there ever was. All the salmon, and whales, and seals lay on the sands because the water was so low. Then the people killed them for food. They had enough food to last them a long time.

When the tide began to rise again, the people were frightened. They feared there would be another flood, so they carried their food back a long distance.

Afterward Raven returned to Nass River and found that people there had not changed their ways. They were dancing and feasting. They asked Raven to join them.

How Raven Stole the Lake (Haida)

After Raven had made the crows black because they had eaten his salmon — crows had always been white before that, they say — he met some people with feathers on their heads and gambling-stick bags on their backs. They said, "What is the matter? "

Raven said, "Oh, my father and mother are dead."

Then they started home with him. These were the Beavers, they say. They were going out to gamble, but turned back on account of him.

The next morning they put their gambling-stick bags upon their backs and started off again. Raven flew around behind a screen. Lo, a lake lay there! In a creek flowing from it was a fish trap. The fish trap was so full of salmon it looked as if someone were shaking it. There were plenty of

salmon in it and in the lake were very small canoes passing each other. Several points of land were red with cranberries.

Raven pulled out the fish trap, folded it together, and laid it down at the edge of the lake. Then he rolled it up with the lake and house, put them under his arm, and pulled himself up into a tree that stood close by. They were not heavy for his arm. He had rolled the lake up just as though it were a blanket. Raven sat in the tree half-way up.

After a while some one came. His house and the lake were not there. After he had looked about him for some time, he looked up. Lo, there sat Raven with their property!

Then the Beavers went quickly to that tree. They began cutting it with their teeth. When it began to fall, Raven went to another one. When that began to fall, he went to another. After the Beavers had cut down many trees in this way, they gave it up. They then travelled about for a long time, they say. After a long time, they found a lake and settled down on it.

Then after Raven had travelled around for a while with the lake, he came to a large open place. He unrolled the lake there. There it lay. He did not let the fish trap or the house go. He kept them to teach the Seaward (mainland) people and the Shoreward (Queen Charlotte Islands) people, they say.

Origin of Light and Fire (Lillooet)

Raven and Sea Gull were friends. Their houses were close together in the Lillooet country. It was dark all over the world at this time, because Sea Gull owned the daylight, which he kept in a box. He never let any of it out except for his own use.

Raven said, "It isn't fair that Sea Gull should have all the daylight. People should have some of it." Therefore Raven planned to get the daylight.

One night he placed thorn branches on the trail between Sea Gull's house and the place where his canoe was fastened. Then he ran to Sea Gull, shouting, "Your canoe has gone adrift! Your canoe has gone adrift!" Sea Gull heard Raven and rushed out of the house in haste. He did not even put on his moccasins; he ran in his bare feet and stepped on the thorns. Then Sea Gull screamed "Ah-ah!" just as sea gulls do now. He shouted to Raven, "Get my canoe! Save my canoe!" Then he went back to his house. He was much excited.

Raven pulled up the canoe and went to the house. Gull spoke of those thorns in his feet. Raven said, "Oh, I can pull them out, if you will let a little daylight out of your box." So Gull sat down beside the box and opened it a little with one hand. Raven began to pull out the thorns with an awl. Soon he said, "I can't see well. Give me more light." Gull opened the box a little more.

Raven pulled out all the thorns but one. He said, "This last one is hard to get out. I shall need more light." When Gull opened the box a little more, Raven gave his arm a push. Thus he knocked down the box and broke it. Then all the daylight rolled out and spread all over the world. Sea Gull was unable to collect it again.

Raven took out the last thorn and went home chuckling.

Now Raven could see very well indeed, and one day he cleaned himself nicely. He combed and oiled his hair, and put on his best robe, and painted his face black. Then he sat on the top of his underground house and looked all over the world. He saw nothing. The third day he changed the paint on his face. That evening he saw signs of smoke. The fourth day Raven changed his face paint again. Now he located the smoke. It was far

away to the south, on the shore of the sea.

Raven had four servants. They all at once entered a small canoe, but it was swamped. Then he tried another. Then he said to his wife, "Go to Sea Gull's house and tell him I need to borrow his canoe." So he started off in Sea Gull's canoe.

Now they paddled downstream until they were close to the house of the people who owned the fire. They planned very quietly. That night they bored a hole under where the baby board hung and stole the baby. Then they ran away.

Now early in the morning the people missed the baby. They knew what had happened. But Raven was too far ahead. They sent out men. Sturgeon, Whale, and Seal searched for Raven's boat, but they could not find him. Other men searched, but only one small fish found Raven's canoe. He tried to stop the runaways by sticking to the paddle, but after a while he got tired and went home. Now Raven reached his own country.

Then the Fire People visited Raven with presents. Four times they came; Raven refused all their gifts. Then they said, "What do you wish?" Raven said, "Fire." Then they said, "Well, why didn't you say that before? "And they were glad, because they had plenty of fire and thought little of its value. So they brought Raven fire, and he gave them back their baby. These Fire People showed Raven how to make fire with dry Cottonwood roots.

Raven said to Sea Gull, "If I had not got the light from you, I could not have seen where the fire was kept."

Raven's Canoe Men (Haida)

Crow made a great feast. He invited all the people, and he invited Raven. But Raven refused. Raven wanted all the feast of hemlock-bark cakes and cranberries.

Before they began eating, Raven ran into the woods. He made rotten trees into ten canoes. Then he put in spruce cones, standing them up along the middle of the canoes. Raven put grass tops into their hands for spears. Raven walked near them, with his blanket wrapped tightly around him. The canoes came around the point, terrible to behold! Men were standing in lines along the middle of the canoes. The people fled at once. They left their feast. Then Raven went into the house and ate the cakes of hemlock bark and cranberries. He ate and he ate! When the canoes landed they were washed about by the waves.

Raven and Moon-woman (Haida)

Raven became the son of Moon-woman. He cried a great deal. When he cried, he said, "Boo-hoo, moon!" Then his mother said, "He talks about a thing beyond his reach, which the supernatural beings own." So Raven began to cry again, "Boo-hoo, moon!"

Then, when Moon-woman's mind was tired out with his noise, she stopped up all the holes in the house. She stopped up the smoke hole, and all the small holes as well. Then she untied the strings of the box. Although they were very strong, she untied them. She did this because the moon was inside the box. Then she took the moon out and let Raven play with it. She did not give it to him; she only let him play with it to quiet him.

After his mother had gone out, Raven took up the moon in his beak. He turned himself into a raven and flew about the house with it. He made himself small. Just before his mother returned, he made himself a child again. Then he again played with the moon.

Then Raven again began crying loudly, when his mother returned. He cried, "Boo-hoo, boo-hoo, smoke hole!" So he cried. "Boo-hoo, boo-hoo, smoke hole!" He cried this way for a long time. Then he tired his mother's mind with his crying, and she opened the smoke hole a little. Raven cried, "Boo-hoo, more! Boo-hoo, more!" for a long time. Then she made the opening in the smoke hole larger, and he kept crying, "Boo-hoo, more!" until she had made it quite large.

Then again Raven played with the moon. Raven cried because he wanted the moon, and his mother did not want to give it to him. When he cried very much, she gave it to him and made that large opening in the smoke hole.

Now at that time it was always dark. Raven did not like darkness.

Now after she had made the smoke hole larger, his mother again went out, and Raven was playing with the moon. Then he put the moon in his beak and flew through the smoke hole with it. Immediately he put the moon under his wing. He perched up on top of the house with the moon under his arm and called like a raven.

Then Raven flew to the bank of the Nass River, where they were

taking olachen. And it was dark. Raven called, "If you will bring me your spruce needles, I will make it light for you." He called the olachen spruce needles. He said that same thing again.

The fishermen replied, "One who always talks is talking about something which the supernatural beings own, and which is beyond his reach."

Thus they made him angry, and he let them see a little of the moon. It became light. Then they all went to him and gave him a great many olachen.

Raven again put the moon under his arm. Flying up with it, he sat on the top of a high mountain. He took the moon out, and threw it down so it broke. He took half of it and threw it up into the sky, and said, "You shall be the moon and shall give light in the middle of the night. He then threw the other half upward and said, "You shall shine in the middle of the day." Then he threw upward the small fragments, and said, "You shall be the stars; when it is clear, they shall see you all during the night."

Fable of the Animals (Karok)

A great many hundred snows ago, Kareya, sitting on the Sacred Stool, created the world. First, he made the fishes in the Big Water, then the animals on the green land, and last of all, Man! But at first the animals were all alike in power. No one knew which animals should be food for others, and which should be food for man. Then Kareya ordered them all to meet in one place, that Man might give each his rank and his power. So the animals all met together one evening, when the sun was set, to wait overnight for the coming of Man on the next morning. Kareya also commanded Man to make bows and arrows, as many as there were animals, and to give the longest one to the animal which was to have the most power, and the shortest to the one which should have least power. So he did, and after nine sleeps his work was ended, and the bows and arrows which he had made were very many.

Now the animals, being all together, went to sleep, so they might be ready to meet Man on the next morning. But Coyote was exceedingly cunning he was cunning above all the beasts. Coyote wanted the longest bow and the greatest power, so he could have all the other animals for his meat. He decided to stay awake all night, so that he would be first to meet Man in the morning. So he laughed to himself and stretched his nose out on his paw and pretended to sleep. About midnight he began to be sleepy. He had to walk around the camp and scratch his eyes to keep them open. He grew more sleepy, so that he had to skip and jump about to keep awake. But he made so much noise, he awakened some of the other animals. When the morning star came up, he was too sleepy to keep his eyes open any longer. So he took two little sticks, and sharpened them at the ends, and propped open his eyelids. Then he felt safe. He watched the morning star, with his nose stretched along his paws, and fell asleep. The sharp sticks pinned his eyelids fast together.

The morning star rose rapidly into the sky. The birds began to sing. The animals woke up and stretched themselves, but still Coyote lay fast asleep. When the sun rose, the animals went to meet Man. He gave the longest bow to Cougar, so he had greatest power; the second longest he gave to Bear; others he gave to the other animals, giving all but the last

Louis Agassiz Fuertes.

to Frog. But the shortest one was left. Man cried out, "What animal have I missed?" Then the animals began to look about and found Coyote fast asleep, with his eyelids pinned together. All the animals began to laugh, and they jumped upon Coyote and danced upon him. Then they led him to Man, still blinded, and Man pulled out the sharp sticks and gave him the shortest bow of all. It would hardly shoot an arrow farther than a foot. All the animals laughed.

But Man took pity on Coyote, because he was now weaker even than Frog. So at his request, Kareya gave him cunning, ten times more than before, so that he was cunning above all the animals of the wood. Therefore Coyote was friendly to Man and his children, and did many things for them.

How Coyote Stole Fire (Klamath)

Long ago men were hungry and unhappy. They were cold. The only fire in the world was on a mountain top, watched by three Skookums. They guarded the fire carefully. Men might steal it and become as strong as they.

Coyote wanted men to be warm and happy. One day he crept to the mountain top and watched the Skookums. He watched all day and all night. They thought he was only a skulking coyote. Coyote saw that one Skookum sat always by the fire. When one went into the tepee, another came out and sat by the fire. Only when the dawn wind arose was there a chance to steal fire. Then Skookum, shivering, hurried into the tepee. She called: "Sister, sister, get up and watch the fire." But the sister was slow.

Coyote went down the mountain side and called a great council of the animals. He knew if he stole fire, the Skookums would chase him. Coyote said the other animals must help him.

Again Coyote skulked to the mountain top. The Skookums saw only a coyote shivering in the bushes. When the dawn wind rose, the Skookum on guard called: "Sister, sister, get up and watch the fire." But the sister was slow. Then Coyote seized the fire and jumped down the mountain side. Quickly Skookum followed him. She caught the tip of his tail in her hand; therefore it is white, even to this day. But Coyote reached Wolf. Wolf seized the fire and leaped down the mountain. Skookum chased Wolf. But Wolf reached Squirrel. Squirrel seized the fire and leaped from branch to branch down the mountain. The fire was so hot it burned the back of his neck. You can see the black spot there, even to this day. The fire was so hot it made Squirrel's tail curl up over his back. Skookum chased Squirrel. But Squirrel reached Frog. Frog took the coals of fire in his mouth and hopped away. Skookum chased Frog. She caught his tail in her hand. Frog jumped away but Skookum kept the tail. That is why frogs have no tail, even to this day. Soon Skookum caught up with Frog again. To save the fire, Frog spit it out on Wood. Wood swallowed it. Skookum did not know how to get the fire out of Wood. But Coyote did. Coyote showed the Indians how to get fire out of Wood by rubbing two dry sticks together, as they do even to this day.

Origin of the Tribes (Chinook)

Long ago, in Lake Cle-el-lum, lived Wishpoosh, the monster beaver. Cle-el-lum was beautiful. It was also full of fish. The animal people wanted to fish there but Wishpoosh killed them. Wishpoosh dragged them into the water and drowned them. Wishpoosh also killed and ate the animal people.

At last Coyote tried to kill him. Coyote fastened a spear to his wrist with a strong cord. Then he began to fish in the lake. Soon Wishpoosh attacked him. Coyote speared the beaver. Then Wishpoosh plunged to the bottom of Cle-el-lum and dragged Coyote with him. But Coyote fought hard with Wishpoosh.

They fought so hard, they tore out the banks of Cle-el-lum. The waters rushed through the break, then through the mountains and down the canon. They rushed into Kittitas Valley. The water formed another lake in Kittitas Valley.

Coyote and Wishpoosh fought so hard they tore out the banks of the new lake. The waters rushed down into the basin of the Cowiche, Nachess, and Atahnum. The water formed a larger lake. Yakima was flooded and a very great lake formed at Toppenish.

Coyote and Wishpoosh fought so hard that they tore out the banks of this very great lake. The waters rushed to the meeting-place of the Yakima, the Snake, and the Columbia Rivers. The waters here formed a very, very great lake.

Coyote and Wishpoosh fought so hard that even the banks of this lake were torn out. Then Wishpoosh dashed down the Great River. Coyote was out of breath. Coyote wanted to stop Wishpoosh. He caught at the trees and stones along the banks of Great River. Nothing could stop Wishpoosh. At last Coyote and the beaver reached the breakers at the mouth of Great River, reached the breakers of the Bitter Waters.

Wishpoosh was very angry. He killed salmon and swallowed them. He killed whales and swallowed them. Coyote saw that Wishpoosh was very strong. Then he remembered that he was Coyote, the wisest and cunningest of all the animals. So Coyote changed himself into a branch, a tree branch. He drifted toward Wishpoosh. Wishpoosh swallowed him.

Then Coyote changed himself back into Coyote again. He took his stone knife. He cut the sinews inside of Wishpoosh. Thus Wishpoosh died.

Now Coyote was very tired. Therefore he asked Muskrat to help him. Together Coyote and Musk- rat pulled the great beaver to land. Then they cut up Wishpoosh. They threw the pieces over the land.

From the head of Wishpoosh, Coyote made the Nez Perces, great in council. From the arms he made the Cayuses, powerful with the bow and war-club. From the legs he made the Klickitats, famous runners. From the ribs he made the Yakimas. From the belly he made the Chinooks, short, fat people, with big stomachs. Coyote at last had only the hair and blood of Wishpoosh. These he flung far up the valley to the east. They became the Snake River Indians, a tribe of war and blood.

Thus Coyote created the tribes. Then he returned up the Columbia.

Now in making the Chinooks and the coast tribes, Coyote forgot to give them any mouth. The god Ecahni, travelling along, noticed this. Then Ecahni called the tribes to him and with a stone knife gave each one a mouth. But for fun Ecahni cut them crooked. He made some mouths very big. Thus the coast tribes have not perfect mouths.

How Ah-ha'-le Stole the Sun (Miwok)

To-to'-kan-no the Sandhill Crane was chief of the Valley People and Ah-ha'-le, the Coyote-man, lived with him. Their country was cold and dark and full of fog.

Ah-ha'-le was discontented and traveled all about, trying to find a better place for the people. After a while he came to the Foothills Country where it began to be light. He went on a little farther and for the first time in his life saw trees, and found the country dry and warm, and good to look at. Soon he saw the Foothills People and found their village. He was himself a magician or witch doctor, so he turned into one of the Foothills People and mingled with them to see what they had and what they were doing. He saw that they had fire, which made light and became Wut'-too the Sun. He saw also that there were both men and women, that the women pounded acorns and cooked acorn mush in baskets, and that everybody ate food. He ate with them and learned that food was good.

When his belly was full he went home and told the chief To-to'-kan-no that he had found a good place where there were people who had the sun and moon and stars, and women, and things to eat. He then asked To-to'-kan-no, "What are we going to do? Are we going to stay down here in the dark and never eat? The people up there have wives and children; the women make acorn soup and other things; the men have light and can see to hunt and kill deer. We live down here in the dark and have no women and nothing to eat. What are we going to do?"

Chief To-to'-kan-no answered; "Those things are not worth having. I don't want the Sun, nor the light, nor any of those things. Go back up there if you want to."

Ah-ha'-le went back to the foothills and did as he had done before, and liked the country and the people. Then he returned and told To-to'-kan-no what he had told him before, and again asked, "What are we going to do? Can't we buy the Sun? The people up there send the Sun away nights so diey can sleep, and it comes back every day so they can see to hunt and get things to eat and have a good time. I like the Sun. Let us buy him."

To-to'-kan-no answered, "What is the matter with you? What would you do with the Sun; how would you use it?" But Ah-ha'-le was not

Ch. Bodmer pinx. ad. nat.　　　　　　Imp. de Bougeard.　　　　　　Beyer sculp.

satisfied. He went back to the Foothills People several times, and the more he saw of the Sun the more he wanted it. But To-to'-kan-no always said he did not want it. Finally however he told Ah-ha'-le that he might go and find out what it would cost.

Ah-ha'-le went and found that the people would not sell it; that if he got it he would have to steal it. And this would be very difficult, for Ah-wahn-dah the Turtle, keeper of the Sun, was most watchful ; he slept only a few minutes at a time and then stood up and looked around; besides, when he slept he always kept one eye open. If Ah-ha'-le moved his foot Ah-wahn'-dah would pick up his bow and arrow. Ah-ha'-le felt discouraged and did not know what to do. He feared that in order to get the Sun he would have to take Ah-wahn'-dah also.

But he decided to try once more, so he went again and turned into a man of the Foothills People. About four o'clock in the afternoon all the hunters went off to hunt deer. Then Ah-ha'-le turned into a big oak limb and fell down on the trail, and wished that Ah-wahn'-dah the Sun's keeper would come along first. And so it happened, for soon Ah-wahn'-dah came along the trail, saw the crooked limb, picked it up, carried it home on his shoulder, and threw it down on the ground. After supper he picked it up again and threw it against the fire, but it would not lay flat for it was very crooked and always turned up. Finally Ah-wahn'-dah threw it right into the middle of the fire. Then he looked all around, but could not see anybody. Ah-ha'-le who was now in the fire did not burn, but kept perfectly still and wished the keeper, Ah-wahn'-dah, would go to sleep.

Soon this happened and Ah-wahn'-dah fell fast asleep. Then Ah-ha'-le changed back into his own form and seized the Sun and ran quickly away with it.

Ah-wahn'-dah awoke and saw that the Sun was gone and called everybody to come quick and find it, but they could not for Ah-ha'-le had taken it down through the fog to the Valley People.

But when the Valley People saw it they were afraid and turned away from it, for it was too bright and hurt their eyes, and they said they could never sleep.

Ah-ha'-le took it to the chief, To-to'-kan-no, but To-to'-kan-no would not have it; he said he didn't understand it; that Ah-ha'-le must make it go, for he had seen how the Foothills People did it.

When To-to'-kan-no refused to have anything to do with the Sun, Ah-ha'-le was disappointed, for he had worked very hard to get it.

Still he said, "Well, I'll make it go."

So he carried the Sun west to the place where the sky comes down to the earth, and found the west hole in the sky, and told Wut'-too to go through the hole and down under the earth and come up on the east side and climb up through the east hole in the sky, and work in two places—to

make light over the Foothills People first, then come on down and make light over the Valley People, and then go through the west hole again and back under the earth so the people could sleep, and to keep on doing this, traveling all the time.

Wut'-too the Sun did as he was told. Then To-to'-kan-no and all the Valley People were glad, because they could see to hunt, and the Foothills People were satisfied too, for they had the light in the daytime so they could see, and at night the Sun went away so all the people could sleep.

After this, when the Sun was in the sky as it is now, all the First People turned into animals.

Coyote and Grizzly
(Nez Perce)

Once there was a grizzly bear who was always angry. One day when travelling through the woods she came upon a band of Indians. She ate them all. In the evening, when she had reached home, she had a bad headache and in the night she became very sick because she had eaten so many Indians. She was sick for a week and almost died. She sent for Coyote to come as a medicine man. But Coyote said to his friends, " I do not care if she dies. It would not hurt me or anybody else. Everybody would be glad of it." But as his wife told him to go in company with others, he finally went to see Old Grizzly.

After a while he came to Old Grizzly's house and made medicine. Then she got well. He told her she was sick from eating too many choke cherries, because he thought all the people would run away if he told the truth and said it was from eating too many Indians. But when the people were gone and he himself was ready to run he told her she had eaten too many Indians.

Old Grizzly jumped up and chased Coyote. He ran up the hills; he ran down the valleys ; he ran through the woods. At last he changed himself into a buffalo eating grass by the trail. Now Grizzly Bear thought she would catch Coyote, no matter into what form he changed himself. So when she saw the buffalo, she started to kill it, but then she saw Coyote's trail running past it. So she followed the trail. When she had gone some ways, Coyote changed himself into his own form again. He called after Grizzly Bear and said, "You are only a foolish old bear. You can never catch me."

When Grizzly Bear heard Coyote's voice, she started after him again.

After a while Coyote changed himself into an old man who had smallpox. He was in a tepee by the trail. His clothes were old and worn. When Grizzly Bear came up, she looked into the house. She asked the man if anyone had passed. He told her a man had crossed the river. She saw a bridge with tracks on it. The bridge was made of willows. Now she thought she could get across on that bridge, so she walked on it. The bridge broke, she fell into the water, and was drowned.

Then Coyote turned himself into his own form and went back to his people. He told them he had killed Grizzly Bear.

Coyote in the Buffalo Country (Flathead)

Coyote took to the trail again. After a while he had nothing to eat. He was nearly starved. He went into a tepee at noon and lay down to rest. He was very weak because he had had nothing to eat. This happened in the Jocko Valley.

Coyote heard some one halloo, but he could not see any one. Then some one called again. After he had looked carefully for some time, Coyote saw Eagle a long ways off.

Eagle said that far away there was a country where there were buffalo all the time. Eagle said, "I am going there, but you cannot. You are too poor."

Then Coyote was angry. Coyote said, "I can go anywhere. I am going there." Coyote started out and in fifteen days he reached the place. It was near Great Falls. There was a big camp there and the chief's name was Bear. The people did not like Bear. When buffalo were killed, Bear would take the best pieces for himself all the good meat and the chunks of fat.

Coyote wanted to be chief himself. So he killed a big buffalo and stripped off all the fat. Then he cut the meat in strips and hung it up to dry. After that he built a big fire and heated some stones red hot.

Bear heard that Coyote had killed a buffalo, so he came to look at the meat. Bear said, "This is nice meat. I will take it."

Coyote said, "I saved some fat for you."

Then Coyote took a red hot stone, wrapped it in fat, and put it in Bear's mouth. Thus Coyote killed Bear. Then the people made Coyote chief.

Now Bear was a great medicine man. Whatever he wished came true. There were many buffalo at Great Falls because Bear had wished it. After Coyote became chief all the buffalo went away. Then the people said, "Coyote is a bad chief."

Coyote went out again to hunt for buffalo. He was all alone and he hunted for five days. But the buffalo were all gone. Coyote was ashamed to go back to the camp so he kept right on.

In a little while Coyote met Wolf. Wolf said, "Where are you going?"

Coyote said, "I am going to travel all over the world."

Wolf went on ahead. Soon Coyote heard some one coming. It was a man with plenty of meat. Coyote lay down by the trail and pretended to be dead. The man stopped. He said, "This is pretty good fur." So he threw Coyote among the meat and went on.

Coyote ate all the meat he could hold. Then he ran away. After a while he met Wolf again. Wolf said, "You look fat. Where did you get meat?"

Coyote told him he had pretended to be dead. He said, "The man wanted me for my fur. Your fur is finer than mine. If you pretend to be dead, you can get meat."

Wolf heard the man coming so he lay down by the trail and pretended to be dead. The man stopped. He said, "This is pretty good fur, but I'll make sure he is dead." Then he hit Wolf with a club. He hit Wolf twice.

Then Wolf jumped up and ran away. Wolf was very angry. He said, "Coyote did this on purpose. I will kill Coyote."

Wolf ran and Coyote ran. After a while Wolf overtook Coyote. Wolf said, "Why did you play that trick on me. Now I will kill you."

Coyote said, "Wait until I tell you something. Then you can kill me."

Wolf said, " What do you want to tell me?"

Coyote said, "There are only two of us. It is not fair for us to fight alone. Let us get others to fight with us. Then it will be like one tribe fighting another."

Wolf agreed. So Wolf went in one direction and Coyote in another. Wolf met Bear. Wolf said, "Come with me and fight Coyote." Then Bear and Wolf went on together.

In a little while they met Mole. Wolf said, "Come with me and fight Coyote." So Wolf and Bear and Mole went on together.

Now Coyote had gone in another direction. He met Cat and Dog. Coyote said, "Come with me and fight Wolf." So Coyote and Cat and Dog went on together.

Now Wolf reached the meeting-place first. He looked up and said, "I see Coyote coming." Coyote was coming with Cat and Dog. Coyote was dressed up, with beaded moccasins and a beaded shirt. Therefore he was a great chief. When the fight began, Coyote with Cat and Dog killed all his enemies. Then Coyote went on alone.

Coyote and the Salmon (Klamath)

Then Coyote went to Klamath River. He found the people very poor. They had no food. The river was full of salmon but the people could not get any. Three Skookums had built a dam to prevent the salmon from coming up the river. So the Skookums had all the fish, but the people had none. Coyote was very angry. Coyote said, "Before many suns, fish shall come up the river. The people shall have all the salmon they need."

Then Coyote went to the mouth of the river. The Skookums saw him. They thought he was only a skulking coyote. Coyote whined for some of their fish. Skookum would not give him any. Coyote came close to their camp. The Skookums drove him away. But Coyote saw where the Skookums kept the key of the dam. That was what he had wanted when he whined for fish.

Next morning, one Skookum started down to open the trap and let in a fish for herself. Coyote ran out of the tepee, jumped between Skookum's feet and tripped her up. Skookum fell and the key fell out of her hand. Then Coyote picked up the key, and went to the dam. Coyote opened the dam and let the fish through. The salmon went upstream into the country of the Cahrocs. Then the people had food to eat.

Afterwards Coyote broke down the dam. Ever since then salmon go every year up that river.

How Coyote was Killed (Clatsop)

Coyote had done many things. Fire he had stolen from Skookums and salmon he had given to the Indians. Therefore Coyote, thinking very highly of himself, wanted to travel to the sky world.

Now Star came every night very close to Coyote. Coyote lived above the clouds, on a mountain top. Therefore Coyote said to Star, "Take me with you." Star only laughed. Thus Coyote was angry. Coyote said every night when Star came, "Take me with you into the sky." But Star only laughed. Then Coyote howled at Star.

At last Star said, "Tomorrow night I will take you to the sky world."

Next night Star came again to the mountain. Star came quite close to Coyote. Then Coyote leaped far and caught on the edge of Star. So they travelled through the sky world. Star climbed higher and higher. Coyote looked down. The tall firs of the forest were only as large as arrows. Then Coyote became cold, travelling high in the sky world. Star was not warm like Sun. Coyote became so cold he could not hold on. His paws slipped and he fell. Coyote fell far to the earth below him. For ten snows he fell. When Coyote struck the earth he was crushed as flat as a willow mat. Thus Coyote was killed.

Wiske-djak and the Geese (Algonquin)

Wiske-djak was always hungry. One time, in the autumn of the year, he stood on the shores of a lake, when clouds of ducks were flying by overhead. Wiske-djak wanted some of those ducks. He thought for a long time. Then he made a small clearing right there on the lake shore, and built quite a large tepee, with a fire in the center. The grassy floor of the tepee was very smooth, so one could dance well there. Wiske-djak made a birch-bark door, with a long center stick to keep the bark spread,

and to prevent the door from opening inward. Now everything was ready.

Wiske-djak went out walking and soon met Duck. "I suppose you will soon be going south," he said. "Yes," said Duck, "and we'll be gone all winter. It's a bit cold up here for us."

"It would be pleasant," said Wiske-djak, "if we all had a dance before you went. Invite your friends, all of them, and Geese and any of the others who go south for the winter. We'll have a dance in my tepee." Duck thought that would be very pleasant

Wiske-djak went back to his tepee, and sat down in the sunshine outside. He got his drum and rattle and began to sing a song of invitation. He sang:

"You will all be gone for a long time. You will all be gone until it is wann again. Let us have a dance before you go."

Thus he sang.

Soon ducks and geese came flying by overhead, and they heard his singing. They alighted on the ground very near the tepee.

Wiske-djak called, "Let us go inside and have a good dance," and he opened the door. In went all the ducks. Wiske-djak mended the fire so it would give very little light

"Now," he said, when he had finished that, "you must all follow the rules of the dance. You must do whatever I call out." So they all began to dance. Geese were there and ducks and a few loons, and Cyngabis was there also. They danced hard, around and around the tepee.

Then Wiske-djak said, " Now close your eyes. Don't open them until I give the order. That is one of the rules of the dance."

The birds all closed their eyes tightly, and as they danced and sang, they made a great deal of noise. Anyone who has seen Indians dance knows that they make much noise. So Wiske-djak caught one fat bird after another, and wrung his neck as he passed him in the dance. No one heard anything at all because of the noise of the dancing.

But after a while Cyngabis thought Wiske-djak was moving around in the dance, so he slipped into a dark corner and opened one eye just a little. At once he saw that Wiske-djak was wringing the neck of the dancers. He called out, "Wiske-djak is killing you! Fly!"

At once the birds all opened their eyes and took wing. They flew very rapidly indeed. But Cyngabis was way over in one corner and he was the very last man to get out. Wiske-djak tried to catch him but he got away.

Now Wiske-djak began to cook the birds for a feast. He built the fire outside the tepee, after poking the earth loose with a stick. Then he buried his birds in the hot earth, with the hot coals above them. Then he went to sleep.

Now some Indians came around the point in a canoe. They saw the smoke of the fire, and they saw something strange lying beside the fire.

Therefore they went nearer.

One Indian said, " Look out, it might be Wiske-djak up to more of his mischief!" But another Indian went ashore, saying, "I'll see who it is and what he is doing." When he came close to the fire, there lay Wiske-djak, sure enough, and sound asleep. But the Indian couldn't see why he should have a big fire on a warm day until he saw ducks' legs sticking out of the earth under the hot coals. At once he went back to his friends and told them all about it

The Indians all jumped out of the canoe. They said, "Ha! We will take Wiske-djak's ducks and geese and eat them ourselves." With their paddles they dug up all the birds, twisted the legs off, and put the leg bones back in the earth. They looked just as Wiske-djak had placed them. Then the Indians paddled off.

Soon Wiske-djak waked up. He got up and looked all around. No one was there. Everything looked just as it had when he went to sleep. He looked at the dying coals, and said, "I guess those birds are pretty well cooked by this time." He went all around the coals, pulling out the ducks legs. They came out very easily. He was surprised. "They must be very tender," he thought. He dug around in the earth, but not one thing did he find. Wiske-djak was disgusted.

Wiske-djak and the Partridges (Algonquin)

Wiske-djak wandered over the swamps and mountains feeling all out of sorts with himself. It was just after the Indians had stolen all his ducks and geese as they cooked in the coals. All at once he came upon a little flock of partridges, just newly hatched. Their mother was away.

"Kwe!" said Wiske-djak. "What are you doing here?"

"Nothing," said the partridges. "Just staying here."

"Where is your mother?" asked Wiske-djak.

"She's away hunting," they said.

"What's your name?" he asked one of them. And then each little partridge had to tell him his name until he came to the very last. "What's your name?" he demanded.

"Suddenly Frightened," answered little partridge.

"Oh, you!" said Wiske-djak. "What can you frighten?" And he picked up a big lump of soft mud and threw it all over the clean little partridges. "What can you frighten now?" he said. Then he walked off.

He walked for a long time until he came to a high mountain. When he had climbed to the very top he found a nice breeze blowing across it.

"This feels good," said Wiske-djak. "I think I'll stay here." And he searched around until he came to a place clear of trees just on the edge of a great chasm. The rock broke straight away for hundreds of feet, and over the edge of the cliff came a delightful breeze. Wiske-djak lay right down there and went to sleep at once.

By this time Old Partridge had got home, and found them all covered over with mud.

"What has happened to you? Where did you go?" she asked.

"Nowhere," said the little partridges.

"Who did this?" asked Old Partridge.

"Wiske-djak came along," said the littlest one. "He asked us a lot of questions, and then he asked us our names. When I told him my name, he said, 'Well, what could you frighten?' and threw mud all over us."

Old Partridge was angry. She cleaned up the children, and washed them and dried them, and gave them their supper. Then she asked them which way Wiske-djak had gone, and she went straight on his trail.

Old Partridge tracked Wiske-djak to the high mountain. Then she kept right on until she reached the high, rocky cliff. There lay Wiske-djak, fast asleep. Old Partridge went close to him, on the upper side of the rock. She spread her wings, went close to his ears, and flapped her wings and gave her warwhoop. Wiske-djak waked up so suddenly he could only see that something terrible was whooping right above him. He moved backward and fell right over the edge of the cliff:.

"Well," said Old Partridge, "now you know what 'suddenly frightened' means."

Wiske-djak and Great Beaver (Algonquin)

Wiske-djak was traveling about, looking for adventures. He never succeeded in anything he tried to do, and he was always hungry. In his travels he came to Turn-back Lake. White men call it Dumoine Lake. He had no canoe, but he was a good swimmer, yet when he came to Turn-back Lake, he found it too broad to swim. Therefore he started to walk around it.

Wiske-djak wanted to hunt beaver. On one side of the lake he came to a high mountain, very round, which looked just like a beaver lodge. And a little way off-shore, in the lake, was a small island, with many grasses. "Hm-m-m, " said Wiske-djak. "This must be the home of Big Beaver." And so it looked, with the great, round lodge and the island of grasses.

Wiske-djak tried to think how to catch Big Beaver. At last he went to the lower end of the lake and broke down the dam, so the water would run off. He lingered there while the lake drained. He even took a nap. When it was low enough for him to get at Big Beaver, he found that Beaver was gone. But as he looked about, he saw Big Beaver just going over the dam. So he began to chase him.

Wiske-djak followed Big Beaver past Coulonge River and the Pembroke Lakes. But when Big Beaver reached the Calumet Chutes, he was afraid to go through and took to the portage. When Wiske-djak got to the lower end of the portage, however, he had lost sight of Big Beaver and started back up the Ottawa River. When he got to the upper end, he saw fresh tracks.

"Somebody has been here," he said very quickly. "I wonder if I might be able to trail him? I might get something to eat."

Wiske-djak followed the tracks to the lower end of the portage, and found they turned toward the upper end, so he raced back there. He did not see any beaver, however, so he turned back again to follow other fresh tracks to the lower end of the portage. Then he saw he had been following his own trail.

Even today one can see Wiske-djak's footprints in the stone on the Calumet portage.

WA-EM-BOESH-KAA

A Chippeway Chief

Wek'-wek's search for his father (Miwok)

Ah-ha'-le the Coyote-man told the people that there were four holes in the sky—one in the north, one in the south, one in the east, and one in the west. In those days Tim-me-la-le the Thunder came out of the north hole in winter and went back about May, just as he does now.

At this time Wek'-wek the Falcon was not yet born. His father, Yi'-yil, had gone far away to the south, where he had been killed before Wek'-wek's birth.

When Wek'-wek was fourteen years old he already had two or three wives, one of whom was Yow'-hah the Mallard Duck. He asked her if she was old enough to have seen his father. She replied, "No."

He then traveled all about and asked all the people who his father was and where he had gone, but no one could tell him. Then he went out to search; he traveled north, south, east, and west, but could find no trace of his father and no one could tell him where he had gone.

Then Wek'-wek transformed himself into a witch doctor and said, "Now I know where my father went, I smell him."

At sundown he came home to Yow'-hah his wife, and when she had fallen asleep he took a forked limb of a tree and put it in the bed beside her. Then he went down into a hole in the ground and came up near the village (thus leaving no tracks). Then he went south.

In the morning Yow'-hah awoke and found the forked limb and pushed it away saying, " What's the matter with my husband?" She asked his other wives if they had seen which way he went—"Which way did our husband go?" she asked.

They replied, "Go away, you live with him, we don't."

Then Yow'-hah went away and cried. She cried for a day or so, but no one could tell her which way Wek'-wek had gone.

She then took a crooked acorn stick and stuck it in the ground and the stick sprang south. Then she knew the way he had gone, and quickly prepared some baskets of food and set out to follow him.

After a while she overtook him, bringing him the food. By this time Wek'-wek was very tired and had fallen down on the side of the trail. He had a partner, Hoo-loo'-e the Dove, who accompanied him. He said to Hoo-loo'-e, "The old woman is coming behind; I am going to shoot her."

But when she came he could not pull the arrow. She went to him and said, "You are hungry; I've brought you food."

He was angry and would not answer. He said to Hoo-loo'-e his partner, "You are hungry, you had better eat."

Hoo-loo'-e replied, "Yes, I think I am hungry."

"Well, eat," said Wek'-wek, and Hoo-loo'-e ate.

Wek'-wek was angry and would not eat. He told his wife to go home and not follow him. He said: "I go to a bad place; I follow my father; nobody can get through the hole in the sky; you go home."

She answered, "No, I'll not go home, I'll follow you."

Then Wek'-wek continued on the trail of his father.

Wek'-wek had an aunt, Ol'-lus muk-ki'-e the Toad-woman. Her husband was O-wah'-to, the big-headed Fire Lizard. He had a fire which he could send to burn people.

Wek'-wek told Hoo-loo'-e his partner to go around another way with Yow'-hah his wife while he stopped to talk to his aunt's husband, O-wah'-to. Again he told his wife to go home, but she would not. Then Wek'-wek went to the place where O-wah'-to lived. He saw his aunt Ol'-lus muk-ki'-e outside, cracking acorns, and went to her to get something to eat.

O-wah'-to, who was inside the house, called out "Who's there?" and his wife answered, "Nobody." Then he heard Wek'-wek take another step, and called out again, "Who's there?" and again his wife answered, "Nobody, only Oo'-choom the Fly." She whispered to Wek'-wek to step very softly and to eat very quickly—to hurry and eat and go. But O-wah'-to heard him and exclaimed, "Somebody is out there sure," and he came out and saw Wek'-wek, and sent his fire to burn him.

Wek'-wek ran and ran as fast as he could and caught up with Hoo-loo'-e and Yow'-hah, but the fire chased them and burnt so quickly and came so fast that they had not time to reach the hole in the sky. So they turned and ran down to the low country and climbed up on a high rock; but the fire kept on and burned the rock. Then they rushed to the ocean, but the fire dashed after them and made the water boil. Then they hastened north to another big rock, as high as a hill, and climbed on top; but the fire pursued and burnt that rock also. Then they climbed up into the sky, but

the fire pressed on and came so close that it singed the tail of Wek'-wek's quiver. Then they ran down into the low country again and found a crack in the ground and all three crawled into it. But the fire came and burnt down into the crack and drove them out.

By this time Wek'-wek's wife, Yow'-hah, had become very tired from so much running, and gave out. She said to her husband, "You are of no account. Why don't you put out that fire? I would like to see you make a pond half a mile wide."

"I'll try," he answered and shot an arrow of the *kow'-woo* wood (the buttonball bush) into the ground and water came up through the hole and continued to rise until they all stood in water, but still the fire beset them and made the water boil. Yow'-hah said she thought she would die. Then Wek'-wek shot an arrow into the ground in another place and a spring of water came and green stuff grew around the edges; but the fire continued and made the water boil as before.

Again Yow'-hah said, "You are of no account; you would die if I had not followed you."

Wek'-wek answered, "All right, you try."

Yow'-hah took a tule and threw it, and a big spring burst out, bordered all around with a broad belt of green tules; and they stepped into the spring and the fire could not reach them—it could not burn the green tules. So the fire went out and there was no more fire. Yow'-hah the old woman had stopped the fire. She was proud of this and said, "You see, if I had stayed at home you would be dead; if I go you will be all right." And the three continued on together.

By and by they came to the hole—the south hole in the sky. Then Wek'-wek said, "You two had better go home, you can't get through the hole."

His wife answered "No," and tried to go through but failed.

Wek'-wek shot an arrow through, but the hole closed so quickly that it caught the arrow and broke it. He again said to the others, "You can't get through." Then he tried and jumped so quickly that he went through. Then Hoo-loo'-e his partner tried, and likewise jumped very quickly and got through, and the sky did not catch him. Then Yow'-hah had to try again. Wek'-wek told her she must go through or go back. But she was too big and too slow. She said, "You will have to take me through." So he went back and got her and put her into his dog-skin quiver and jumped through with her. As they passed through, the hole closed and caught her feet and crushed them flat—that is why all ducks have flat feet.

Now all three were through.

In the south, beyond the hole in the sky, were other people. They had two chiefs, Ho'-ho the Turkey Buzzard, and Koo'-choo, a huge shaggy beast of great strength and fierceness. Tap-pitch'-koo-doot the Kingbird lived there, and Hok'-ke-hok'-ke also.

Before Wek'-wek arrived, Captain Ho'-ho the Buzzard said to the people, "I dreamed that a north Indian is coming—the son of Yt'-yil, the man we burned. Everybody watch; maybe we shall have a good time again." So everybody watched.

After a while the watchers saw Wek'-wek coming. They saw him come through the hole. Then they ran back and told the people. This made the people happy, and they made ready to play the ball game.

When Wek'-wek reached the village he saw his father's widow there crying, with her hair cut short in mourning. He asked her, "Did my father die here?"

"Yes," she answered, and added, "Your father had plenty of money when he lost the game, but the chiefs Koo'-choo and Ho'-ho would not take the money; they were playing for his life; they wanted to burn him. Old Koo'-choo made a circle around the fire and made your father stand in the middle, and told him not to die too soon. After he had been burning a little while Koo'-choo asked how far the fire had burned, and Yi'-yil answered, 'To my knees, I'm going to die.'

"'No, don't die yet,' said Koo'-choo; and he asked again, ' How far has the fire burned now?'

"Yi'-yil answered, 'To my belly, and I'm going to die now.'

"'No, don't die yet,' said Koo'-choo, and he asked again, 'How far has the fire burned now?'

"' To my heart,' replied Yi'-yil, 'and I'm going to die now.'

"'No, no,' again said Koo'-choo, 'don't die yet; how far has the fire burned now?'

"'To my shoulders and I'm going to die,' said Yi'yil.

"'No, don't die yet; how far has the fire burned now?'

"'To my mouth, and I'm going to die,' answered Yi'-yil.

"'No, not yet, there's plenty of time yet,' said Koo'-choo; 'how far has it burned now?'

"'To my eyes, it's burning my eyes now and I'm going to die,' replied Yi'-yil.

"'No, no,' said Koo'-choo, 'don't die yet;' and when he saw that the fire had reached the top of Yi'-yil's head he asked again and for the last time, 'How far has it burned now?'

"There was no reply, and he knew, and all the people knew, that Yi'-yil was burned to death and was dead."

This is what Yi'-yil's widow, who had seen the burning, told Wek'-wek.

Wek'-wek was very angry; he knew that the people wanted to burn him as they had burned Yi'-yil his father; and he made up his mind what he would do. He left his wife Yow'-hah with Koo'-choo and the others and told her to entertain them. He then asked his father's widow which way they had taken his father to play the ball game. She told him, and he

followed his father's trail. He found gopher holes in the trail, and holes the people had made for the ball to fall into so he would lose the game, and he filled them up. He came back over Koo'-choo's trail by daylight and found it all right—all the holes filled up and no holes left.

When he returned he found that the two firemen, Lol'-luk the Woodrat and No-put'-kul-lol the Screech Owl, had the fire all ready to burn him, but he said nothing.

Early next morning they all set out down the trail to play the ball game. Wek'-wek played so fast that old Koo'-choo became very tired and nearly gave out. He shot out a terrible skunk-like smell to make Wek'-wek sick, but Wek'-wek kept ahead and was not harmed.

Wek'-wek won the game and came back first; all the others were tired and Koo'-choo came in half dead.

When they had returned, Yow'-hah, Wek'-wek's wife, told Wek'-wek to burn Koo'-choo first.

Koo'-choo said to Wek'-wek: "You have won the game; everybody will bring you money; here is the money; you take it."

Wek'-wek answered, "No, I'll not take it. You would not take my father's money; you took his life."

Then they brought two more sacks full of money, but Wek'-wek pushed it away. He seized the two wicked chiefs, Koo'-choo and Ho'ho; he seized them by their arms and threw them into the fire that had been prepared for him, and took the others in the same way and threw them all in the fire. Some ran away and tried to hide, but Wek'-wek went after them and brought them back and threw them in the fire—men, women, and children—and burned them all. He then called the firemen to come—Lol'-luk the Woodrat and No-put'-kul-lol the Screech Owl—but they cried and refused to come. Then he took his bow and arrow and shot them and pitched them into the fire and they were burned like the rest.

The only people not burned were two witch doctors—Pel-pel'-nah the Nuthatch and Choo-ta-tok'-kwe-lah the Red-headed Sapsucker. They lived in the big ceremonial house and never came out; they never ate and never drank. Wek'-wek asked them, "Shall I come in?"

They answered, "Yes."

Wek'-wek went inside and said: "You two are witch doctors; you never eat and never drink and never see people. Do you think you can make my father live again? I'll pay you. I want to see my father. I want to see what he is like."

They answered that they would try. One said to the other: "We will try; yes, we must try; but how shall we do it?" Then they took a jointed rod of *la-hah* (the wild cane) and put Yi'-yil's burnt bones in the hollow inside, and put three or four feathers on the outside, like an arrow. Then Choo-ta-tok'-kwe-lah asked Wek'-wek for his bow, and took it and shot

the cane arrow high up into the air; and when it was way up, Yi'-yil came slowly out of the hole in the end and sailed around and around, coming lower and lower, till he came down where the others were.

Then Wek'-wek asked him, "Are you my father? You don't look as I supposed."

Yi'-yil answered, "Yes, I'm Yi'-yil your father."

Wek'-wek said, "I've burned all the people here. Will you go home with me? Are you sure you are my father?"

"Yes," answered Yi'-yil, "I'm your father and I'll go home with you."

"All right," said Wek'-wek, "Let's go."

After a while, when they had gone a little way, Wek'-wek turned and said, "I think you had better not go with me. You look queer—only half like us. You go to the other side of the mountain down on the coast" (meaning Oo'-yum-bel'-le, Mount Diablo). Then Yi'-yil went back into the cane arrow, and Wek'-wek, his wife Yow'-hah, and his partner Hoo-loo'-e returned through the hole in the sky that they had gone through on their way south.

When they were on the other side, Wek'-wek said to his wife: "Old woman, you may have to run again. I'm going to kill O-wah'-to, my uncle-in-law, who chased us with fire and tried to destroy us when we were here before." So he sent Yow'-hah and Hoo-loo'-e ahead and told them to wait for him while he proceeded to O-wah'-to's place. He went there and shot O-wah'-to with an arrow and killed him dead the first shot.

Then they continued on, and when they had gone a few miles, they came to another fireman, whose name was Hos-sok'-kil-wah. Wek'-wek sent his wife and partner ahead as before while he went alone to fight Hos-sok'-kil-wah. He took an arrow with a point of white flint stone, and shot and killed Hos-sok'-kil-wah, who at once turned into the white flint fire rock. And so they continued, Wek'-wek killing all the people on the way.

Wek'-wek's search for his sister (Miwok)

After Wek'-wek, Hoo-loo'-e, and Yow'-hah had returned home, Wek'-wek said, "I have heard that I once had a sister; where is my sister?"
No one answered.

Then Wek'-wek slept and dreamed. Then he went off alone to the north and told no one.

Wek'-wek had a nephew, Ah'-ut the Crow. Ah'-ut asked the people, "Where is my uncle?" No one answered. Then Ah'-ut said he would find him, and he also set out for the north. Finding that he could not catch up with Wek'-wek, he shot an arrow and the arrow went over Wek'-wek's head and fell just beyond.

Wek'-wek knew who had shot it, and said, "Who told my nephew?"

When Ah'-ut came up, Wek'-wek asked, "Why do you follow me? I'm searching for my sister; you go home."

"No," answered Ah'-ut, "I'll go with you."

Then Wek'-wek's brothers, two little hawks, who also had been following, overtook Wek'-wek and Ah'-ut and all went on together.

After a while they found the rancheria. It was in a big cave about two miles below Koo-loo'-te Wek'-wek sent one of his little brothers into the cave. He went in and on one side of the entrance saw O-hum'-mah-te the Grizzly Bear, and on the other side He-le'-jah the Mountain Lion, but saw nothing of the sister.

Then Wek'-wek sent in the other brother. When he returned he said some one was inside cooking acorns ; he had seen a woman cook the acorn soup by putting into the basket hot quail eggs instead of hot stones. He said also that farther back in the cave was something that looked like a sharp rock.

Then Ah'-ut the Crow said he would go in. When he found the woman cooking with the quail eggs he picked them up and took off the shells and ate all the eggs. Then he asked the woman, "Is my uncle's sister here?"

"Yes," she answered, "but you can't go in."

But he did go in, and when he came to He-le'-jah the Mountain Lion, he said, "You are good to eat," and shot him with an arrow and killed him. Then he turned to O-hum'-mah-te the Grizzly Bear and said the same to

him, and killed him also and pulled him out. Then he went in farther and saw the Sharp Rock and shot it also and killed it, and picked up his arrow and put it back in his quiver. Then he went still farther in and found Wek'-wek's sister. She was old and naked and shriveled—nothing but bare bones—for no one had given her anything to eat.

Ah'-ut returned and told Wek'-wek he could now go in, and Wek'-wek went in. When he saw his sister without clothes and all bones he felt badly and cried. Then he took her out and helped her walk, and cooked some acorns and fed her. Then he sent her home with his brothers.

Wek'-wek's visit to the Underworld People (Miwok)

After Wek'-wek had sent his sister home he stayed near the caves below Koo-loo'-te and dug holes in the sand and found roots and seeds that were good to eat. In digging he came to a very deep hole which led down under the world; he went down this hole and when he reached the underworld found other people there, and got a wife with a little boy. Besides his wife there were To-to'-kon the Sandhill Crane, Wah'-ah the Heron, Cha-poo'-kah-lah the Blackbird, and others.

To-to'-kon the Sandhill Crane was chief. When he saw Wek'-wek he said, "What shall we do with this man; he is lost; we had better kill him."

Wek'-wek saw a man make ready with his bow and arrow, and invited him to come and eat. The man came and ate, and when his belly was full went back.

Captain To-to'-kon said, "I didn't send you to eat, but to kill him." Then he sent another, and Wek'-wek asked him also to come and eat, and he did as the other had done. Then Captain To-to'-kon sent two men together to kill him, but Wek'-wek called them both to come and eat, and they did so. Then To-to'-kon was angry; he sent no more men but went himself and took his bow and arrow.

Wek'-wek said to him, "Come in," whereupon To-to'-kon shot his arrow but missed.

Then Wek'-wek came out and faced the people. They fired all their arrows but could not kill him. Wek'-wek said, "You can't kill me with arrows. Have you a pot big enough to hold me?"

"Yes," they answered.

"Then set it up and put me in it," he said.

And they did as they were told and put Wek'-wek in the hot pot and put the cover on. When he was burned they took out the burnt bones and buried them in the ground.

Ah'-ut the Crow missed his uncle and went to his uncle's partner, Hoo-loo'-e, who was in the hole crying, and asked where Wek'-wek was. Hoo-loo'-e pointed down the hole. Ah'-ut went down and found the rancheria of the underworld people and killed them all. He then asked Wek'-wek's wife where Wek'-wek was. She answered that the people had burned and buried him.

Wek'-wek stayed in the ground five days and then came to life; he came out and asked his wife where the people were. She told him that Ah'-ut had come and killed them all. "That is too bad," he exclaimed, "I wanted to show them what kind of man I am." Then he said she should stay there and he would take the boy and go home.

She answered, "All right."

Then he shot his arrow up through the hole and caught hold of it, and held the boy also, and the arrow carried them both up to the upper world.

A Legend of Manabozho (Ojibwa)

Manabozho made the land. The occasion of his doing so was this. One day he went out hunting with two wolves. After the first day's hunt one of the wolves left him and went to the left, but the other continuing with Manabozho he adopted him for his son. The lakes were in those days peopled by spirits with whom Manabozho and his son went to war. They destroyed all the spirits in one lake, and then went on hunting. They were not, however, very successful, for every deer the wolf chased fled to another of the lakes and escaped from them. It chanced that one day Manabozho started a deer, and the wolf gave chase. The animal fled to the lake, which was covered with ice, and the wolf pursued it. At the moment when the wolf had come up to the prey the ice broke, and both fell in, when the spirits, catching them, at once devoured them.

Manabozho went up and down the lake-shore weeping and lamenting. While he was thus distressed he heard a voice proceeding from the depths of the lake.

"Manabozho," cried the voice, "why do you weep?"

Manabozho answered—

"Have I not cause to do so? I have lost my son, who has sunk in the waters of the lake."

"You will never see him more," replied the voice; "the spirits have eaten him."

Then Manabozho wept the more when he heard this sad news.

"Would," said he, "I might meet those who have thus cruelly treated me in eating my son. They should feel the power of Manabozho, who would be revenged."

The voice informed him that he might meet the spirits by repairing to a certain place, to which the spirits would come to sun themselves. Manabozho went there accordingly, and, concealing himself, saw the spirits, who appeared in all manner of forms, as snakes, bears, and other things. Manabozho, however, did not escape the notice of one of the two chiefs of the spirits, and one of the band who wore the shape of a very large snake was sent by them to examine what the strange object was.

Manabozho saw the spirit coming, and assumed the appearance of a stump. The snake coming up wrapped itself around the trunk and

6878. OTOSSAWAY, AN OBJIBWA CHIEF.

squeezed it with all its strength, so that Manabozho was on the point of crying out when the snake uncoiled itself. The relief was, however, only for a moment. Again the snake wound itself around him and gave him this time even a more severe hug than before. Manabozho restrained himself and did not suffer a cry to escape him, and the snake, now satisfied that the stump was what it appeared to be, glided off to its companions. The chiefs of the spirits were not, however, satisfied, so they sent a bear to try

what he could make of the stump. The bear came up to Manabozho and hugged, and bit, and clawed him till he could hardly forbear screaming with the pain it caused him. The thought of his son and of the vengeance he wished to take on the spirits, however, restrained him, and the bear at last retreated to its fellows.

"It is nothing," it said; "it is really a stump."

Then the spirits were reassured, and, having sunned themselves, lay down and went to sleep. Seeing this, Manabozho assumed his natural shape, and stealing upon them with his bow and arrows, slew the chiefs of the spirits. In doing this he awoke the others, who, seeing their chiefs dead, turned upon Manabozho, who fled. Then the spirits pursued him in the shape of a vast flood of water. Hearing it behind him the fugitive ran as fast as he could to the hills, but each one became gradually submerged, so that Manabozho was at last driven to the top of the highest mountain. Here the waters still surrounding him and gathering in height, Manabozho climbed the highest pine-tree he could find. The waters still rose. Then Manabozho prayed that the tree would grow, and it did so. Still the waters rose. Manabozho prayed again that the tree would grow, and it did so, but not so much as before. Still the waters rose, and Manabozho was up to his chin in the flood, when he prayed again, and the tree grew, but less than on either of the former occasions. Manabozho looked round on the waters, and saw many animals swimming about seeking land. Amongst them he saw a beaver, an otter, and a musk-rat. Then he cried to them, saying—

"My brothers, come to me. We must have some earth, or we shall all die."

So they came to him and consulted as to what had best be done, and it was agreed that they should dive down and see if they could not bring up some of the earth from below.

The beaver dived first, but was drowned before he reached the bottom. Then the otter went. He came within sight of the earth, but then his senses failed him before he could get a bite of it. The musk-rat followed. He sank to the bottom, and bit the earth. Then he lost his senses and came floating up to the top of the water. Manabozho awaited the reappearance of the three, and as they came up to the surface he drew them to him. He examined their claws, but found nothing. Then he looked in their mouths and found the beaver's and the otter's empty. In the musk-rat's, however, he found a little earth. This Manabozho took in his hands and rubbed till it was a fine dust. Then he dried it in the sun, and, when it was quite light, he blew it all round him over the water, and the dry land appeared.

Thus Manabozho made the land.

Manabozho in the Fish's Stomach (Ojibwa)

One day Manabozho said to his grandmother—

"Noko, get cedar bark and make me a line whilst I make a canoe."

When all was ready he went out to the middle of the lake a-fishing.

"Me-she-nah-ma-gwai (king-fish)," said he, letting down his line, "take hold of my bait."

He kept repeating these words some time; at last the king-fish said—

"What a trouble Manabozho is! Here, trout, take hold of his line."

The trout did as he was bid, and Manabozho drew up his line, the trout's weight being so great that the canoe was nearly overturned. Till he saw the trout Manabozho kept crying out—

"Wha-ee-he! Wha-ee-he!"

As soon as he saw him he said—

"Why did you take hold of my hook? Esa, esa! Shame, shame! you ugly fish."

The trout, being thus rebuked, let go.

Manabozho let down his line again into the water, saying—

"King-fish, take hold of my line."

"What a trouble Manabozho is!" cried the king-fish. "Sun-fish, take hold of his line."

The sun-fish did as he was bid, and Manabozho drew him up, crying as he did so—

"Wha-ee-he! Wha-ee-he!" while the canoe turned in swift circles.

When he saw the sun-fish, he cried—

"Esa, esa! You odious fish! Why did you dirty my hook by taking it in your mouth? Let go, I say, let go."

The sun-fish did as he was bid, and on his return to the bottom of the lake told the king-fish what Manabozho had said. Just then the bait was let down again near to the king, and Manabozho was heard crying out—

"Me-she-nah-ma-gwai, take hold of my hook."

The king-fish did so, and allowed himself to be dragged to the surface, which he had no sooner reached than he swallowed Manabozho and his canoe at one gulp. When Manabozho came to himself he found he was in his canoe in the fish's stomach. He now began to think how he should

escape. Looking about him, he saw his war-club in his canoe, and with it he immediately struck the heart of the fish. Then he felt as though the fish was moving with great velocity. The king-fish observed to his friends—

"I feel very unwell for having swallowed that nasty fellow Manabozho."

At that moment he received another more severe blow on the heart. Manabozho thought, "If I am thrown up in the middle of the lake I shall be drowned, so I must prevent it." So he drew his canoe and placed it across the fish's throat, and just as he had finished doing this the king-fish tried to cast him out.

Manabozho now found that he had a companion with him. This was a squirrel that had been in his canoe. The squirrel helped him to place the canoe in the proper position, and Manabozho, being grateful to it, said—

"For the future you shall be called Ajidanneo (animal tail)."

Then he recommenced his attack on the king-fish's heart, and by repeated blows he at last succeeded in killing him. He could tell that he had effected this by the stoppage of the fish's motion, and he could also hear the body beating against the shore. Manabozho waited a day to see what would happen. Then he heard birds scratching on the body, and all at once the rays of light broke in. He could now see the heads of the gulls, which were looking in at the opening they had made.

"Oh!" cried Manabozho. "My younger brothers, make the opening larger, so that I can get out." The gulls then told one another that Manabozho was inside the fish, and, setting to work at once to enlarge the hole, they, in a short time, set him free. After he got out Manabozho said to the gulls—

"For the future you shall be called Kayoshk (noble scratchers), for your kindness to me."

The Sun and the Moon (Ojibwa)

There were once ten brothers who hunted together, and at night they occupied the same lodge. One day, after they had been hunting, coming home they found sitting inside the lodge near the door a beautiful woman. She appeared to be a stranger, and was so lovely that all the hunters loved her, and as she could only be the wife of one, they agreed that he should have her who was most successful in the next day's hunt. Accordingly, the next day, they each took different ways, and hunted till the sun went down, when they met at the lodge. Nine of the hunters had found nothing, but the youngest brought home a deer, so the woman was given to him for his wife.

The hunter had not been married more than a year when he was seized with sickness and died. Then the next brother took the girl for his wife. Shortly after he died also, and the woman married the next brother. In a short time all the brothers died save the eldest, and he married the girl. She did not, however, love him, for he was of a churlish disposition, and one day it came into the woman's head that she would leave him and see what fortune she would meet with in the world. So she went, taking only a dog with her, and travelled all day. She went on and on, but towards evening she heard some one coming after her who, she imagined, must be her husband. In great fear she knew not which way to turn, when she perceived a hole in the ground before her. There she thought she might hide herself, and entering it with her dog she suddenly found herself going lower and lower, until she passed through the earth and came up on the other side. Near to her there was a lake, and a man fishing in it.

"My grandfather," cried the woman, "I am pursued by a spirit."

"Leave me," cried Manabozho, for it was he, "leave me. Let me be quiet."

The woman still begged him to protect her, and Manabozho at length said—

"Go that way, and you shall be safe."

Hardly had she disappeared when the husband, who had discovered the hole by which his wife had descended, came on the scene.

"Tell me," said he to Manabozho, "where has the woman gone?"

"Leave me," cried Manabozho, "don't trouble me."

"Tell me," said the man, "where is the woman?" Manabozho was silent, and the husband, at last getting angry, abused him with all his might.

"The woman went that way," said Manabozho at last. "Run after her, but you shall never catch her, and you shall be called Gizhigooke (day sun), and the woman shall be called Tibikgizis (night sun)."

So the man went on running after his wife to the west, but he has never caught her, and he pursues her to this day.

Manabozho the Wolf (Ojibwa)

Manabozho set out to travel. He wished to outdo all others, and see new countries, but after walking over America, and encountering many adventures, he became satisfied as well as fatigued. He had heard of great feats in hunting, and felt a desire to try his power in that way.

One evening, as he was walking along the shores of a great lake, weary and hungry, he encountered a great magician in the form of an old wolf, with six young ones, coming towards him. The wolf, as soon as he saw him, told his whelps to keep out of the way of Manabozho.

"For I know," said he, "that it is he we see yonder."

The young wolves were in the act of running off, when Manabozho cried out—

"My grandchildren, where are you going? Stop, and I will go with you."

He appeared rejoiced to see the old wolf, and asked him whither he was journeying. Being told that they were looking out for a place where they could find the most game, and best pass the winter, he said he should like to go with them, and addressed the old wolf in these words—

"Brother, I have a passion for the chase. Are you willing to change me into a wolf?"

The old wolf was agreeable, and Manabozho's transformation was effected.

He was fond of novelty. He found himself a wolf corresponding in size with the others, but he was not quite satisfied with the change, crying out—

"Oh! Make me a little larger."

They did so.

"A little larger still," he cried.

They said—

"Let us humour him," and granted his request.

"Well," said he, "that will do." Then looking at his tail—

"Oh!" cried he. "Make my tail a little longer and more bushy."

They made it so, and shortly after they all started off in company, dashing up a ravine. After getting into the woods some distance, they fell in with the tracks of moose. The young wolves went after them,

Manabozho and the old wolf following at their leisure.

"Well," said the wolf, "who do you think is the fastest of my sons? Can you tell by the jumps they take?"

"Why," replied he, "that one that takes such long jumps; he is the fastest, to be sure."

"Ha, ha! You are mistaken," said the old wolf. "He makes a good start, but he will be the first to tire out. This one who appears to be behind will be the first to kill the game."

Soon after they came to the place where the young ones had killed the game. One of them had dropped his bundle there.

"Take that, Manabozho," said the old wolf.

"Esa," he replied, "what will I do with a dirty dog-skin?"

The wolf took it up; it was a beautiful robe.

"Oh! I will carry it now," said Manabozho.

"Oh no," replied the wolf, who at the moment exerted his magic power. "It is a robe of pearls."

From that moment he lost no opportunity of displaying his superiority, both in the hunter's and magician's art, over his conceited companion.

Coming to a place where the moose had lain down, they saw that the young wolves had made a fresh start after their prey.

"Why," said the wolf, "this moose is poor. I know by the tracks, for I can always tell whether they are fat or not."

They next came to a place where one of the wolves had tried to bite the moose, and, failing, had broken one of his teeth on a tree.

"Manabozho," said the wolf, "one of your grandchildren has shot at the game. Take his arrow. There it is."

"No," replied he, "what will I do with a dirty tooth?"

The old wolf took it up, and, behold! it was a beautiful silver arrow.

When they overtook the young ones, they found they had killed a very fat moose. Manabozho was very hungry, but, such is the power of enchantment, he saw nothing but bones, picked quite clean. He thought to himself—

"Just as I expected. Dirty, greedy fellows!"

However, he sat down without saying a word, and the old wolf said to one of the young ones—

"Give some meat to your grandfather."

The wolf, coming near to Manabozho, opened his mouth wide as if he had eaten too much, whereupon Manabozho jumped up, saying—

"You filthy dog, you have eaten so much that you are ill. Get away to some other place."

The old wolf, hearing these words, came to Manabozho, and, behold! before him was a heap of fresh ruddy meat with the fat lying all ready prepared. Then Manabozho put on a smiling-face.

"Amazing!" cried he. "How fine the meat is!"

"Yes," replied the wolf; "it is always so with us. We know our work, and always get the best. It is not a long tail that makes a hunter."

Manabozho bit his lip.

They then commenced fixing their winter quarters, while the young ones went out in search of game, of which they soon brought in a large supply. One day, during the absence of the young wolves, the old one amused himself by cracking the large bones of a moose.

"Manabozho," said he, "cover your head with the robe, and do not look at me while I am at these bones, for a piece may fly in your eye."

Manabozho covered his head, but, looking through a rent in the robe, he saw all the other was about. At that moment a piece of bone flew off and hit him in the eye. He cried out—

"Tyau! Why do you strike me, you old dog!"

The wolf said—

"You must have been looking at me."

"No, no," replied Manabozho; "why should I want to look at you?"

"Manabozho," said the wolf, "you must have been looking, or you would not have got hurt."

"No, no," said Manabozho; and he thought to himself, "I will repay the saucy wolf for this."

Next day, taking up a bone to obtain the marrow, he said to the old wolf—

"Cover your head, and don't look at me, for I fear a piece may fly in your eye."

The wolf did so. Then Manabozho took the leg-bone of the moose, and, looking first to see if the old wolf was well covered, he hit him a blow with all his might. The wolf jumped up, and cried out—

"Why do you strike me so?"

"Strike you?" exclaimed Manabozho. "I did not strike you!"

"You did," said the wolf.

"How can you say I did, when you did not see me. Were you looking?" said Manabozho.

He was an expert hunter when he undertook the work in earnest, and one day he went out and killed a fat moose. He was very hungry, and sat down to eat, but fell into great doubts as to the proper point in the carcass to begin at.

"Well," said he, "I don't know where to commence. At the head? No. People would laugh, and say, 'He ate him backward!'"

Then he went to the side.

"No," said he, "they will say I ate him sideways."

He then went to the hind-quarter.

"No," said he, "they will say I ate him forward."

At last, however, seeing that he must begin the attack somewhere, he commenced upon the hind-quarter. He had just got a delicate piece in his mouth when the tree just by began to make a creaking noise, rubbing one large branch against another. This annoyed him.

"Why!" he exclaimed, "I cannot eat when I hear such a noise. Stop, stop!" cried he to the tree.

He was again going on with his meal when the noise was repeated.

"I cannot eat with such a noise," said he; and, leaving the meal, although he was very hungry, he went to put a stop to the noise. He climbed the tree, and having found the branches which caused the disturbance, tried to push them apart, when they suddenly caught him between them, so that he was held fast. While he was in this position a pack of wolves came near.

"Go that way," cried Manabozho, anxious to send them away from the neighbourhood of his meat. "Go that way; what would you come to get here?"

The wolves talked among themselves, and said, "Manabozho wants to get us out of the way. He must have something good here."

"I begin to know him and all his tricks," said an old wolf. "Let us see if there is anything."

They accordingly began to search, and very soon finding the moose made away with the whole carcass. Manabozho looked on wistfully, and saw them eat till they were satisfied, when they left him nothing but bare bones. Soon after a blast of wind opened the branches and set him free. He went home, thinking to himself—

"See the effect of meddling with frivolous things when certain good is in one's possession!"

How Glooscap Found the Summer (Mi'kmaq)

In the long ago, when the Indians lived in the early red light of the morning, Glooscap, the Great Chief, went very far to the north, where all was ice.

At last he came to a wigwam, and there he found a giant—a great giant, for he was Winter. Glooscap entered the wigwam; he sat down. Then Winter gave him a pipe; he smoked, and the giant told him tales of the olden times.

The charm of the Frost was upon him, and while the Giant Winter talked, the Great Chief nodded and then fell asleep. He slept for six months. Then the charm left him, and he awoke and went upon his journey. He hastened toward the south, and at every step it grew warmer, and by and by the flowers sprang up and talked with him.

At last the Great Chief came to where all the little folk were dancing in the forest. Their queen was Summer, the most beautiful of all women. The Great Chief seized her, and by a clever trick he kept her. For he cut a moose hide into a long cord ; and as he ran away with Summer, he left the end of the cord trailing behind him.

Then the little folk, the fairies of the Light, pursued him. They saw the cord trailing, and caught it. But as the Great Chief ran, he let the long cord run out, and left the fairies far behind.

The Chief traveled on until he came once more to the lodge of the Giant Winter. But now he could not be charmed. He was stronger than Winter; for he brought the Summer with him.

The Giant Winter welcomed the Great Chief for he hoped to freeze him again into slumber. But now this time the Chief talked. And as he talked, great drops of sweat began to run down old Winter's face. The Chief talked on, and the Giant Winter began to melt. He melted, and melted, until at last he had quite melted away.

Then everything awvke. The grass grew; the fairies came out; the snow melted and ran down the rivers, carrying away the dead leaves.

Then the Great Chief left Summer with them, and went home.

How Glooscap Conquered his Enemies (Mi'kmaq)

Once, in the long ago, the Great Chief Glooscap lived on an island called Aja-lig-un-mechk. With him were many Indians, who had the names and natures of animals and birds ; and who had the power to take the form of these animals and birds when they wished. All of these Indians had magical power, but they were not so powerful as the Great Chief. So they were jealous of him; and at last they determined to go away and leave him alone, and to take with them little Marten and the grandmother, who lived with Glooscap. They thought that if they left him alone on the island he would soon die—for they did not know the power of the Master.

They waited until Glooscap went into the forest on a long journey. Then they made everything ready, and stole away to the canoes. But just then Glooscap came back out of the forest, and saw that the grandmother and Marten were gone. He followed their tracks to the shore. There he saw Winpe, a mighty sorcerer, his greatest enemy, pushing off with them in a canoe. They were still near the shore, and Glooscap called loudly to the grandmother: "Noogumee, send me back my dogs." These dogs were very small, no larger than mice. The grandmother took a small wooden dish, and put it into the water, and placed the dogs upon it, and they floated back to the shore. Glooscap took up the dogs, and put them into his pocket, and returned to his wigwam; and his enemy, Winpe, paddled away across the water with Marten and the grandmother.

A long time passed, but Glooscap did not pursue his enemy. Some say that it was three months; some say, seven years. Why he did this no one knows. Perhaps it was so that he could gain greater power ; perhaps he had other work to do; perhaps he wished to let his enemies suffer. But when the right time came, the Great Chief took his dogs and went down to the shore. He stood and looked far out to sea, and then he began to sing a magic song. It was the song that all the whales obeyed. He watched, and soon a small whale arose far off in the sea. He had heard the Great Chief's call, and he came swimming to him. When the whale was close to the shore, Glooscap rested one foot upon the whale's back to try his weight; but he was very heavy, and the whale sank down in the water.

How Glooscap Conquered his Enemies (Mi'kmaq)

"You are not large enough," said the Great Chief. "Return to your home in the ocean."

Then Glooscap sang his magic song once more. Soon there came Bootup, the largest whale in all the ocean. Glooscap stepped upon her back, and she bore him swiftly away over the sea.

Now as Bootup sped across the ocean she began to think that if she went so fast she might run upon the shore, or come to a place where the water was shallow, and she could not get out again. This was just what Glooscap wanted her to do.

As Bootup came near the shore she kept asking Glooscap whether he could see the land. But Glooscap always answered:

"No."

Then Bootup would go on again as fast as she could. But soon Bootup saw clam shells under the water, and she was more afraid than ever. She called out:

"My grandson, does not the land show itself in the distance like a bow-string?"

"We are still far from land," said Glooscap. So she went on, until the water was so shallow that they could hear the clams singing.

Now these clams were enemies of Glooscap; and they were singing to Bootup, urging her to throw him into the sea and drown him. She could not understand what they said, so she asked Glooscap:

"My grandson, what are the clams singing?"

"They tell you to hurry me on as fast as you can," said Glooscap. So Bootup swept on through the water, thinking that the clams were urging her to hurry—until all at once she found herself high and dry on the shore. Then she was terribly frightened, and she began to cry out:

"Alas, my grandchild, you have been my death. I shall never again swim in the sea."

And Glooscap answered:

"Do not fear, Noogumee."

He gave one push of his bow against the great whale and she was sent far out to sea. Then Bootup was glad once more. She lighted her pipe, and went sailing happily home, smoking as she went.

Glooscap now began to search for the trail of Winpe and Marten and the grandmother; and after a long time he came to a deserted wigwam, and there he found a small birch-bark dish, which had belonged to Marten. Glooscap examined it, and saw that it had been there for seven years — although some say it was only three months. So by this he knew how long Winpe had been away from this place. The Great Chief followed the trail eastward and found another deserted wigwam, where Winpe had been. Near this wigwam there was a wretched lodge, and in

54061 ANGRY BEAKER, AN OJIBWA BRAVE

it a poor, helpless-looking old woman, doubled over with age. She was really an artful sorceress, Glooscap's deadly foe, who was determined to kill him. The Great Chief knew this at once. The old woman asked him to help her, and Glooscap pretended to do everything she asked, but while he busied himself in the lodge, he put her into a deep sleep by his magic, and went his way.

Soon the sorceress awoke, and when she found that she had been outwitted, and that Glooscap's contempt for her was so great that he had scorned even to destroy her, she was furious; and in her rage, she pursued him, determined to be avenged.

The Great Chief was in no danger, and therefore he had no fear. He carried in his bosom his two little dogs. These dogs were no larger than mice, but they could immediately assume the size and fury of the largest animals. As soon as the sorceress came near him, Glooscap took the little dogs from his pocket, and said to them:

"When I command you not to growl, spring upon her, and the more loudly I call you off, the more furiously must you tear her."

When the sorceress saw the little dogs take on their giant forms, and heard their fierce growls, she was frightened and shrank back from them.

"Call off your dogs!" she shouted.

The Master called out to the dogs to be quiet, but the more he shouted, the more furious they became. They rushed at the sorceress, and destroyed her.

Glooscap now journeyed on until he came to the top of a high mountain. In the distance he saw a large wigwam, where two old wizards, who hated him, lived. These wizards had two daughters.

When the wizards perceived by their magical power that the Great Chief, the enemy of all evil-doers, was near, they sent their daughters out to meet him. They gave them strings of bear's meat to put around his neck—as was the custom—but this was magical meat which, once around his neck, would have strangled him to death.

When Glooscap saw the maidens coming to meet him, he knew who they were, and what their intentions were. He gave his dogs the magical word, and let them go. As soon as they began to growl at the sorcerers, Glooscap commanded them to be quiet, saying:

"These maidens are my sisters." But the dogs rushed on, and tore them to pieces.

Glooscap took the magical meat that was intended to kill him, and went to the wigwam; and looking in at the door, he threw it around the old man's neck. Then he went on, leaving the sorcerer strangled by the magical meat.

Then Glooscap made his way toward the shore; but he must travel over a mountain where there was a narrow pass, guarded by a Kookwes, a terrible giant. This Kookwes managed to entrap all who passed, whether man or beast.

When he saw Glooscap approaching, he said: "Now I shall have a capital dinner!" Glooscap gave his dogs the magical word, and went boldly into the pass to face the Kookwes. The Kookwes rushed at Glooscap to kill him, but the dogs with a bound seized the giant by the throat, and killed him.

The Great Chief knew that he had now destroyed all the sorcerers that beset his way, and that he must next attack Winpe, the greatest enemy of all. He set out once more upon his journey, and soon reached the sea. He followed along the shore, stopping at the old camping places of Winpe. He always examined the little bark dishes that were left behind, and these told him that he was rapidly gaining upon his enemy.

Soon he came to a place where Winpe had crossed the water. The Great Chief stood upon the shore, and sang his magical song which the whales obeyed. At once a whale answered his call, and carried him swiftly across to the other shore. Glooscap hastened on, and followed along the shore until he found that he was but a three days' journey behind his enemy, the terrible sorcerer, Winpe.

Again he must cross the water; and again he sang the magical song which the whales obeyed. A great whale appeared, and soon carried him safely to the other side. Glooscap now came to the place where Winpe had camped the night before. Then he hurried, speeding over the ground with mighty strides, and before long he overtook his old housekeeper, weak and tottering with hunger and abuse. She was carrying Marten on her back, for he was so weak that he could walk no farther. Winpe and his family were far ahead, but the grandmother did not dare to try to escape, for she feared the power of the wicked sorcerer.

Marten, who had his face turned backward, was the first to spy Glooscap following them.

"My elder brother, help us! Give us food!" he called.

"The Chief is not here," the grandmother said sadly. "We left him far, far, behind."

Marten soon caught another glimpse of Glooscap, and called again for food. The grandmother looked back this time, and when she saw the Master, she was so overjoyed that she fainted. When she became conscious, Glooscap stood beside her. She began to weep, and to tell him how cruel Winpe had been to them.

"Think no more of it," said Glooscap; "They will soon have their punishment."

They traveled along together until they came to the place where Winpe was camping, and then Glooscap said to Marten:

"I will hide here, and when Winpe sends you for water, make it unclean. And then when he scolds you, throw the baby into the fire and run to me."

Marten did just as Glooscap told him. He put mud and filth into the water, and when Winpe saw it, he said:

"Horrors! What terrible water! Go and get some that is clean."

Marten tossed the baby into the fire, and ran as fast as he could toward the place where Glooscap was hiding, calling out:

"Nsesaho! My elder brother! Come and help me."

Winpe pursued him, vowing vengeance, crying exultingly:

"Your brother cannot help you. He is far, far away, where we left him; and though you bum the world, I will seize you and kill you."

On ran Marten with Winpe close behind him, until they came almost to Glooscap's hiding-place. Then the Great Chief sprang up and stood before Winpe. The sorcerer stopped short, and challenged Glooscap to fight. Then he stepped back, and summoned all his magical powers. He

could have smoked it unless he were a magician. They passed the pipe around, and every one smoked. The brothers blew the smoke through their nostrils, but when the pipe came to Glooscap, he filled it full again, lighted it, and with one pull burned all the tobacco into ashes, and blew all the smoke through his nostrils at one puff.

Then the brothers were angry, and said again, "This is indeed a great magician, but he shall be tried before he goes, and that bitterly."

They tried again to smoke with him. They closed the wigwam and hoped to smother him in smoke. But Glooscap sat and smoked away as though he were on a mountain top. At last the brothers could bear the smoke no longer, and they said, "This is idle. Let us go and have a game of ball."

The place where they were to play was on a plain, and Glooscap saw that the ball with which they played was a hideous skull. It was alive and snapped at his heels when it rolled. If he had been as other men, and had been bitten so, it would have taken off his foot. But Glooscap laughed and said, "So this is the game you play. Good! But let us each have a ball."

With that he stepped to a tree on the bank of the river, and broke off the end of a bough. At once this turned into a skull ten times more terrible than the other.

The giants ran before this horrible ball; but it pursued them, and they fled from the field.

Then the Great Chief stamped upon the sand, and the waters arose and flooded the place, and streams and rivers poured from the mountain side. The whole land trembled with the roar. Then the Great Chief sang a magic song which changes all beings, and all the wicked sorcerers were transformed into sharks.

How Glooscap was Conquered by Wasis (Mi'kmaq)

In the long ago it came to pass, when Glooscap had conquered all his enemies — the Kewahqu', the giants and sorcerers, and the M'Teoulin, magicians, and the Pamola, the evil spirit of the night, and all kinds of ghosts, witches, devils, cannibals, and goblins, he began to think upon what he had done, and he wondered whether his work on earth were finished. And he spoke these thoughts to a woman, who was clever and ready of tongue. But she replied, "Not so fast. Master, for there yet remains one whom no one has ever conquered, nor got the better of in any way, and who will remain unconquered to the end of time."

"And who is he?" asked the Master.

"It is the mighty Wasis," the woman replied; "and there he sits. And I warn you that if you meddle with him you will be in sore trouble."

Now Wasis was the Baby! And he sat upon the floor, sucking a piece of maple sugar, greatly contented, troubling no one.

As the lord of Men and Beasts had never married, nor had a child, he knew nothing of the way of managing children. But, like all such people, he felt very certain that he knew all about it. So he turned to the baby with a sweet smile, and bade the little one come to him.

The Baby smiled back at the Great Chief, but he did not budge.

Then the Master spoke sweetly, and made his voice like the sound of a summer bird, but it was of no avail, for Wasis sat still and sucked his maple sugar, and looked at Glooscap with untroubled eyes.

And then the Master frowned as in great anger, and spoke in an awful voice, and ordered Wasis to come crawling to him at once. Baby burst out into wild tears and screams — but for all that he did not move one inch.

Then the Master, since he could do but one thing more, tried that. Glooscap had recourse to magic. He used his most dreadful spells; he sang the songs which raise the dead, and scare the devils, and drive the witches to their graves, and bend the great pines in the forest. And all the time Wasis sat and looked at him admiringly, and seemed to think it interesting — but for all that he did not stir.

So in despair Glooscap gave up, for he had no more arts. And Wasis, sitting on the floor in the sunshine, went, "Goo! Goo!"

And to this day, when you see a baby, quite content, saying "goo! goo!" and crowing, you may be sure he is thinking of the time when he overcame the Great Chief, who had conquered all the world.

For of all beings that have ever been, since the world began, Baby alone is invincible.

Origin of the Thunder Bird (Klamath)

Long, long ago, Toe-oo-lux, South Wind, traveled to the north. There Toe-oo-lux met Quoots-hooi, the giantess. Toe-oo-lux said, "I am hungry. Give me something to eat."

Quoots-hooi said, "I have nothing to eat. You can get food by fishing."

So South Wind dragged the net. He caught tanas-eh-ko-le. He caught a little whale. South Wind took his stone knife to kill the whale.

Then the giantess said, "Use a sharp shell. Do not use your knife. Slit tanas-eh-ko-le down the back. Do not cut him crossways."

South Wind pretended not to hear. South Wind cut the whale across the back. Suddenly the fish changed into an immense bird. The bird's wings darkened the sun. The flapping of its wings shook the earth. This bird was the Thunder Bird. He flew to the north and lighted on Swal-al-a-host, near the mouth of Great River.

Then South Wind and the giantess traveled north to find him. One day, picking berries, Quoots-hooi found the nest of Thunder Bird. The nest was full of eggs.

Quoots-hooi broke one egg. It was not good, so she threw it down the mountain side. Before it reached the valley it became an Indian. Quootshooi threw down other eggs. Each egg became an Indian. That is how the Chehalis Indians were created.

Indians never cut the first salmon across the back. If they did, the salmon would not run. Always Indians slit the first salmon down the back.

Turtle and the Thunder Bird (Ojibwa)

Once Turtle was living all alone in a lake. Several times he was hit by something. When he came out to see what it was, he could see nothing at all. One day he was struck again. He thought he would ask someone to help him. When he came out of the water, he went into the woods. He cried, "Who will help me? Who will help me?"

Deer ran out from among the shrubs and said, "I will help you."

"Come on," said Turtle, "let me see how you can fight." Deer started to fight a tree and broke his horns.

Turtle said, "Oh, you will not last long enough." He left Deer and again called out, "Who will help me?"

Bear came out and said, "I will help you."

Turtle said, "Let me see how you can fight."

Bear started to fight a tree, but he was so clumsy jumping around, that Turtle said, "Oh, you won't last long if you have to fight the giant I am after."

Turtle again began to call, "Who will help me?"

He called this as he came to a little swamp, and he heard small voices saying, "We will."

"Come out and show me how you can fight," said Turtle. And behold! a crowd of little Turtles came out and began to fight him. Soon Turtle cried, "You're the very people I am looking for." So he led them to the lake where he lived and left them just outside. Then he went home. Soon a big stone fell down upon the little turtles and killed them all. When Turtle ran out to see what had happened, he saw a big bird overhead.

Turtle ran to his neighbor who had ducked into the water. He asked, "What bird was that?"

Muskrat answered, "That is the Thunder Bird and I am very much afraid of him."

Ever since that day Turtle has stayed in the water when there was a thunderstorm.

Why Lightning Strikes the Trees (Thompson River)

Thunder Bird was angry with people and tried to drown the whole world, but he could not make the water rise high enough, so some of the people escaped. Then Thunder Bird shot arrows at them. He really did hurt many, but all the people ran away and hid in a cave.

Then Turtle came out. He shouted out to Thunder Bird, "You cannot kill people. Your arrows fly wild. Shoot at the trees and rocks; perhaps you can hit them." Turtle mocked Thunder.

Thunder said, "Oh, yes, I do strike people. I have killed many of them!"

Turtle said at once, "Well, then, prove it by killing me." So he drew his shell down tight and moved about very carelessly, not hiding at all, while Thunder shot many arrows at him. They only glanced off his thick shell.

Then Thunder Bird believed that he really could not hit people, so now he shoots his arrows at trees and rocks. But if people stand under a tree in a storm, it is likely that Thunder will hit them.

The Last of the Thunderbirds (Inuit)

Long, long ago there were many thunderbirds living in the mountains, but at last there were only two left. These birds made their home on the round top of a mountain overlooking the Yukon. They hollowed out a great basin on the summit for a nest, and from the rocky rims they could look down upon a village upon the river bank.

From this perch the thunderbirds, looking like a black cloud, would soar away, bringing back to their young a reindeer in their talons. Sometimes with a great noise like thunder they swooped down upon a fisherman in his kayak and carried him away. The man would be eaten by the young birds, and the kayak broken to bits in the nest. Every fall the young birds flew away into the northland, but the old birds remained in the nest. They had carried away so many fishermen that only the most daring would go out on the great river. One day when a fisherman went to look at his traps, he cautioned his wife not to leave the house for fear of the thunderbirds. During the morning, she needed fresh water and started for the river. A noise like thunder filled the air, a black shadow fell over her, and a thunderbird darted down upon her.

When the fisherman returned to his house, people of the village told him of the thunderbird. He made no answer. He took his bow and quiverful of war arrows and started for the mountain. When he reached the rim of the great nest, he looked in. The old birds were away. The nest was full of young eagles with fiery, shining eyes and shrill cries. The hunter fitted a war arrow, the string twanged, and the arrow killed a young thunderbird. So the hunter killed them all.

The hunter hid behind a great rock near the nest. When the old birds came home, the thunder of their wings was heard even across the great river; their cries of rage frightened the villagers on the river's bank. The mother bird swooped down upon the hunter beside the rock. Quickly he fitted a war arrow, the string twanged, and the arrow bit deep into her throat. Then the mother bird, flapping her wings so that the hills shook, flew away to the northland.

The father bird circled overhead and then swooped down upon the hunter. He crouched below the rocks and the thunderbird's great talons caught only the rock. The hunter fitted a war arrow in his bow, the string twanged, and the heavy war arrow bit deep under his great wing. Spreading his wings like a black cloud in the sky, the thunderbird flew away to the northland.

The Magic Birth of Nenebuc and His Four Brothers (Ojibwa)

There were two people living, a man and his wife, who had an only daughter. When she was twelve years old, the age of puberty, she was taken over a hill and was kept there in a camp alone for twelve days, neither eating nor drinking, in order that she might have a dream. If she should eat or drink, she would have no dream. If, while she was dreaming, a panther came alone, she would be very strong. So her parents kept her there. The girl dreamed of the sun, so she could not look at the sun any more, for if she did so, she would have to go away from her parents and live with the sun. When the girl had had this dream, she went back to her parents and her father asked her, "What have you been dreaming?" "I am very sorry, but I have dreamed of the sun, so I cannot ever look at the sun again," replied his daughter. "Well, now it is too bad, but you mustn't look at the sun," said her father. "You stay here all the time. Don't look at the sun, that's all."

The girl used to get water at the shore and stay there a long time. One day in March, she went to the water hole, broke the ice and looked into the water. In so doing, she made a mistake, for there was no cloud in the sky and the sun was shining brightly near the horizon, so that, early in the morning, she looked at the sun. She brought the water back in a birch bark pail and placed it inside the wigwam, but she could not sit down. "What is the matter?" said her father. "Why, I looked at the sun," answered his daughter. "Well, good-bye, you've got to live with the sun now," said her father. Then the girl and her parents shook hands and she went away to live with the sun, and is there yet. Before she went away she said to her father, "You will see your grandchildren before long." Then she told him to put his wooden dish upside down before the fire and to leave it there four days and four nights and to look under it every morning. Then she went to live with the sun.

So the old man put the dish upside down before the fire. The first morning he lifted the edge of the dish, looked under, and there he saw Nenebuc, the child of the sun, sitting. The next morning he did the same thing and he saw Nenebuc's brother sitting with him. He kept doing this the third, fourth, and fifth mornings, until there were Nenebuc and his

four brothers all sitting under the dish. Then the old man picked up the dish. One of the brothers, the second brother, had horns on his head and the old man said to him, "You won't stay here. You go to the west." Then he sent one brother to the east, one to the south, and one to the north. So Nenebuc, the eldest of the five, was left. The old man told him to attend to the world and to keep the winds going just right lest the water get stagnant and bad. Then Nenebuc stayed, and his four brothers started to the four parts of the earth.

One day Nenebuc asked his grandfather, "Where have I been born? Had I a mother like other people?" His grandfather would not tell him, but his grandmother told him that he had been found. This appeared queer to Nenebuc and he thought to himself, "The other people have mothers, but I have none. I must find out." So he took a whetstone and, scraping it on a rock, he asked it, "Have I any mother?" "Yes, you have a mother," replied the whetstone and then it told him his story. Then Nenebuc told his grandfather, "I have a mother and four brothers besides. The whetstone told me so."

Soon Nenebuc began growing larger and he thought it strange that he had not been sent out into the world like his brothers, so he asked his grandfather for what reason he had kept him. His grandfather told him that he had kept him at home so that when he became old and feeble Nenebuc would be able to help him, cut wood for him, and hunt for him. This satisfied Nenebuc and he used to help his grandfather in many ways, spearing fish for him in calm days, hunting for him, and doing many other things. He never got into any mischief and he grew very fast.

Nenebuc Tempers the Wind (Ojibwa)

One summer Nenebuc was unable to get fish for the whole summer on account of the high winds. The people almost starved, and then Nenebuc became very angry. He did not like to see his grandfather starving and his anger was aroused against the West Wind for blowing so much. So he told his grandfather that he was going to kill the West Wind for this, but the old man said to him, "Don't kill him. Make him let the wind blow a while and then stop, so that everything will be all right, but don't kill him." "Well, I won't be long away and I'll punish my brother," replied Nenebuc.

So he went away and finally met his brother, the one with the two horns, who lived in the west. Nenebuc hammered him soundly with a club and broke one of his horns. This hurt him, but did not kill him. Then

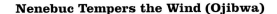

Nenebuc Tempers the Wind (Ojibwa)

Nenebuc said, "Don't blow so hard any more. You don't care for your grandfather, but I do and I fear he and the people will starve." Then he arranged things with his brother and went back. After this he went fishing and found it calm with only a little puff of wind now and then. Then the West Wind told his three brothers not to blow, for if they did Nenebuc would come and kill them. The winds became frightened at this and did not blow at all, and because of this the water grew thick and stagnant and Nenebuc was unable to fish. Then his grandfather said, "We are going to die. There is no wind and the water is bad. Did you kill the West Wind?" "No," said Nenebuc. "I will go and see him and tell him to send the wind once in a while, not too often but just right." So Nenebuc went to his brother, the West Wind, and said to him, "I came here to tell you that I want a little wind once in a while, but not too much." Then everything was arranged satisfactorily. Shortly after this Nenebuc's grandparents died and were heard of no more.

Nenebuc Prepares a Great Feast (Ojibwa)

After this Nenebuc began travelling again. One time he feasted a lot of animals. He had killed a big bear, which was very fat and he began cooking it, having made a fire with his bow-drill. When he was ready to spread his meat, he heard two trees scraping together, swayed by the wind. He didn't like this noise while he was having his feast and he thought he could stop it. He climbed up one of the trees and when he reached the spot where the two trees were scraping, his foot got caught in a crack between the trees and he could not free himself.

When the first animal guest came along and saw Nenebuc in the tree, he, the Beaver, said "Come on to the feast, Nenebuc is caught and can't stop us." And then the other animals came. The Beaver jumped into the grease and ate it, and the Otter did the same, and that is why they are so fat in the belly. The Beaver scooped up the grease and smeared it on himself, and that is the reason why he is so fat now. All the small animals came and got fat for themselves. Last of all the animals came the Rabbit, when nearly all the grease was gone only a little left. So he put some on the nape of his neck and some on his groin and for this reason he has only a little fat in those places. So all the animals got their fat except Rabbit. Then they all went, and poor Nenebuc got free at last. He looked around and found a bear's skull that was all cleaned except for the brain, and there was only a little of that left, but he couldn't get at it. Then he wished himself to be changed into an ant in order to get into the skull and get enough to eat, for there was only about an ant's meal left.

Nenebuc Gets Caught in the Bear's Skull (Ojibwa)

Then he became an ant and entered the skull. When he had enough he turned back into a man, but he had his head inside the skull; this allowed him to walk but not to see. On account of this he had no idea where he was. Then he felt the trees. He said to one, "What are you?" It answered, "Cedar." He kept doing this with all the trees in order to keep his course. When he got too near the shore, he knew it by the kind of trees he met. So he kept on walking and the only tree that did not answer promptly was the black spruce, and that said, "I'm Se'segandak" (black spruce). Then Nenebuc knew he was on low ground. He came to a lake, but he did not know how large it was, as he couldn't see. He started to swim across. An Ojibwa was paddling on the lake with his family and he heard someone calling, "Hey! There's a bear swimming across the lake." Nenebuc became frightened at this and the Ojibwa then said, "He's getting near the shore now." So Nenebuc swam faster, and as he could understand the Ojibwa language, he guided himself by the cries. He landed on a smooth rock, slipped and broke the bear's skull, which fell off his head. Then the Ojibwa cried out, "That's no bear! That's Nenebuc!" Nenebuc was all right, now that he could see, so he ran off, as he didn't want to stay with these people.

190

Picture Credits